Network Type/Feature	Description	Page
	**Installing a VoIP terminal adapter**—Learn how to connect the VoIP terminal adapter into your home network.	80
	**Home phone wiring**—Learn how to connect your Internet phone service into the phone wiring in your house.	90
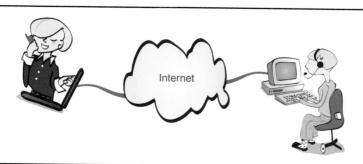	**Troubleshooting**— Understand what to do if your Internet phone service is not working as you expected.	107
	**VoIP Chat service**—Learn how to use VoIP on your laptop or computer to chat with friends and family over the Internet.	121

Internet Phone Services Simplified

An illustrated guide to understanding, selecting, and implementing
VoIP-based Internet phone services for your home

Jim Doherty

Neil Anderson

Illustrations by Nathan Clement

Cisco Press
800 East 96th Street
Indianapolis, IN 46240

Internet Phone Services Simplified

Jim Doherty

Neil Anderson

Copyright© 2006 Cisco Systems, Inc.

Cisco Press logo is a trademark of Cisco Systems, Inc.

Published by:
Cisco Press
800 East 96th Street
Indianapolis, IN 46240 USA

Printed in the United States of America 1 2 3 4 5 6 7 8 9 0

First Printing April 2006

Library of Congress Cataloging-in-Publication Number: 2005936930

ISBN: 1-58720-162-3

Warning and Disclaimer

This book is designed to provide information about Internet telephony services and applications. Every effort has been made to make this book as complete and as accurate as possible, but no warranty or fitness is implied.

The information is provided on an "as is" basis. The authors, Cisco Press, and Cisco Systems, Inc. shall have neither liability nor responsibility to any person or entity with respect to any loss or damages arising from the information contained in this book or from the use of the discs or programs that may accompany it.

The opinions expressed in this book belong to the author and are not necessarily those of Cisco Systems, Inc.

Trademark Acknowledgments

All terms mentioned in this book that are known to be trademarks or service marks have been appropriately capitalized. Cisco Press or Cisco Systems, Inc. cannot attest to the accuracy of this information. Use of a term in this book should not be regarded as affecting the validity of any trademark or service mark.

Corporate and Government Sales

Cisco Press offers excellent discounts on this book when ordered in quantity for bulk purchases or special sales.

For more information please contact: U.S. Corporate and Government Sales: 1-800-382-3419 corpsales@pearsontechgroup.com

For sales outside the U.S. please contact: International Sales international@pearsoned.com

Feedback Information

At Cisco Press, our goal is to create in-depth technical books of the highest quality and value. Each book is crafted with care and precision, undergoing rigorous development that involves the unique expertise of members from the professional technical community.

Readers' feedback is a natural continuation of this process. If you have any comments regarding how we could improve the quality of this book, or otherwise alter it to better suit your needs, you can contact us through email at feedback@ciscopress.com. Please make sure to include the book title and ISBN in your message.

We greatly appreciate your assistance.

Publisher
Paul Boger

Editor-in-Chief
John Kane

Cisco Representative
Anthony Wolfenden

Cisco Press Program Manager
Jeff Brady

Production Manager
Patrick Kanouse

Senior Development Editor
Chris Cleveland

Copy Editor
John Edwards

Technical Editors
Doug Foster
Bradley Mitchell

Editorial Assistant
Katie Linder

Cover Designer
Louisa Adair

Book Designer and Compositon
Mark Shirar

Indexer
Tim Wright

Proofreader
Christy Parrish

CISCO SYSTEMS

Corporate Headquarters
Cisco Systems, Inc.
170 West Tasman Drive
San Jose, CA 95134-1706
USA
www.cisco.com
Tel: 408 526-4000
800 553-NETS (6387)
Fax: 408 526-4100

European Headquarters
Cisco Systems International BV
Haarlerbergpark
Haarlerbergweg 13-19
1101 CH Amsterdam
The Netherlands
www-europe.cisco.com
Tel: 31 0 20 357 1000
Fax: 31 0 20 357 1100

Americas Headquarters
Cisco Systems, Inc.
170 West Tasman Drive
San Jose, CA 95134-1706
USA
www.cisco.com
Tel: 408 526-7660
Fax: 408 527-0883

Asia Pacific Headquarters
Cisco Systems, Inc.
Capital Tower
168 Robinson Road
#22-01 to #29-01
Singapore 068912
www.cisco.com
Tel: +65 6317 7777
Fax: +65 6317 7799

Cisco Systems has more than 200 offices in the following countries and regions. Addresses, phone numbers, and fax numbers are listed on the **Cisco.com Web site at www.cisco.com/go/offices.**

Argentina • Australia • Austria • Belgium • Brazil • Bulgaria • Canada • Chile • China PRC • Colombia • Costa Rica • Croatia • Czech Republic Denmark • Dubai, UAE • Finland • France • Germany • Greece • Hong Kong SAR • Hungary • India • Indonesia • Ireland • Israel • Italy Japan • Korea • Luxembourg • Malaysia • Mexico • The Netherlands • New Zealand • Norway • Peru • Philippines • Poland • Portugal Puerto Rico • Romania • Russia • Saudi Arabia • Scotland • Singapore • Slovakia • Slovenia • South Africa • Spain • Sweden Switzerland • Taiwan • Thailand • Turkey • Ukraine • United Kingdom • United States • Venezuela • Vietnam • Zimbabwe

About the Authors

Jim Doherty is the director of marketing and programs with Symbol Technologies' industry solutions group. Prior to joining Symbol, Jim worked at Cisco Systems, where he led various marketing campaigns for IP telephony and routing and switching solutions. Jim has 17 years of engineering and marketing experience across a broad range of networking and communications technologies. Jim is the coauthor of *Cisco Networking Simplified* and *Home Networking Simplified* and the author of the "Study Notes" section of *Cisco CCNA Exam #640-607 Flash Card Practice Kit.* Jim is a former Marine Corps sergeant; he holds a B.S. degree in electrical engineering from N.C. State University and an M.B.A. from Duke University.

Neil Anderson is a senior manager in enterprise systems engineering at Cisco Systems and is currently responsible for enterprise wide-area networking, branch-office networking, and teleworking systems architectures. Neil has more than 20 years of diverse telecom experience, including public telephone systems, mobile telephone systems, IP networks, wireless networking, and home networks. Neil has held roles in research and development, systems engineering, and technical marketing. Neil is the coauthor of *Home Networking Simplified.* At Cisco Systems, Neil leads the development of network systems architectures, including voice over IP (VoIP), wireless LAN (WLAN), and security technologies, for enterprise and small-business customers. Neil holds a bachelor's degree in computer science.

About the Technical Reviewers

Doug Foster is a customer solutions manager in the sales field marketing group with Cisco Systems and currently works in the area of packet voice, video, and data convergence. In his 30 years of technical and management experience in companies such as John Deere, Alcatel, Cisco, and private business, Doug has been a significant contributor to the evolution of the Internet and has many stories to tell about its early days. Doug has architected and installed international networks, and he was responsible for the migration of John Deere's worldwide SNA business network into a multiprotocol intranet in the mid-1980s. As a result of his work, Doug was asked by the U.S. Department of Defense to speak at Interop '88 on how "John Deere built tractors using TCP/IP." This was nearly a decade before most businesses began to leverage the value of the Internet and e-commerce applications. Doug has a BSME from Iowa State University and lives in Cary, North Carolina, with his wife Cindy. When not busy with work or family—daughters Erin and Amber, son-in-law Jeremy, and grandson Jake—Doug devotes his free time to writing his first book (*Convince Me!*) and to sea kayaking.

Bradley Mitchell writes for the wireless/networking site at About.com where he has produced online tutorials and reference content on computer networking topics for six years. Bradley is also a senior software engineer at Intel Corporation. During the past 12 years at Intel, he has developed, validated, and administered a wide range of network hardware/software systems, published research papers, and developed patents. Bradley obtained his bachelor's degree from M.I.T. and has a master's degree in computer science from the University of Illinois.

Dedications

Jim Doherty: I dedicate this book to Ken Doherty, Phil Doherty, Paul Doherty, Dave Doherty, Joanne Grover, Matt Doherty, and Robert Doherty—the best bunch of potential kidney donors a boy could ever hope for.

Neil Anderson: I dedicate this book to my two beautiful daughters, Courtney and Jillian. Study hard kids. You might need to support your dad someday when he is no longer able to control his bodily functions.

Acknowledgments

The authors would like to thank the following people:

- The fine folks at Cisco Systems and Linksys Networks who provided us with gear, technical assistance, and support; some really smart folks at Cisco Systems who put up with our technical questions: Stuart Hamilton, Joel King, and Steve Schubert; our outstanding publication team who keeps us on task: John Kane, Chris Cleveland, Patrick Kanouse, Katherine Linder, and the entire Cisco Press staff.

- The talented, knowledgeable, and highly entertaining Geek Squad team who protected our readers and will try their best not to make fun of us when they troubleshoot our designs: Chief Inspector Robert Stephens and the many Geek Squad agents who provided insight and commentary.

- Our illustrator Nathan Clement, who is somehow able to figure out exactly what we want even when it is not what we ask for.

- Michele Helies at Vonage whom we are indebted to for her persistence, commitment, and putting up with our pestering.

A very special thanks to our technical reviewers Doug Foster and Bradley Mitchell. Somehow these guys were able to wade through our random, raw writings and help shape them into something worth reading.

Jim Doherty would like to thank: Neil Anderson, my coauthor and friend, and my wonderful family, Katie, Samantha, and Conor, for their never-ending support and inspiration.

Neil Anderson would like to thank: My family, who continues to put up with my disappearances from normal family life so that I can write this stuff. Oh yeah, I would also like to thank Jim Doherty for being my friend and coauthor. May you once again duel on the streets of Tokyo with umbrellas.

Contents at a Glance

Foreword   xiv

Introduction   xv

Part I   Internet Telephony Fundamentals   2

Chapter 1   Traditional Phone Systems   3

Chapter 2   Voice over IP (VoIP)   15

Chapter 3   Advantages of Broadband Phone Services   25

Chapter 4   Knowing Your Limits   33

Chapter 5   From the Geek Squad Files   45

Part II   Choosing an Internet Phone Service   48

Chapter 6   Inventory of Broadband Phone Services   49

Chapter 7   Selecting an Internet Phone Service   55

Chapter 8   Selecting VoIP Equipment   67

Chapter 9   From the Geek Squad Files   73

Part III   Going VoIP at Home   76

Chapter 10   Connecting the VoIP Equipment   77

Chapter 11   Making VoIP Accessible Throughout Your Home   87

Chapter 12   Using Wireless Networks to Extend VoIP   103

Chapter 13   Troubleshooting: Can You Hear Me Now?   107

Chapter 14   From the Geek Squad Files   117

Part IV   VoIP Chat Services   120

Chapter 15   VoIP Chat Services   121

Chapter 16   Using Skype and Google Talk   129

Chapter 17   The Future of Telephony   139

Chapter 18   From the Geek Squad Files   145

Glossary   147

Index   153

Contents

Foreword   xiv

Introduction   xv

Part I   Internet Telephony Fundamentals   2

Chapter 1   Traditional Phone Systems   3

In the Beginning   3

Rise of the Machines   5

Ma Bell   8

Breaking Up the Happy Family   9

Mobile Telephone System   11

Internet   13

Consolidate, Merge, and Acquire   13

Important Things to Know About the PSTN   14

Chapter 2   Voice over IP (VoIP)   15

Circuit Switching and Packet Switching   15

How VoIP Works   17

VoIP Signaling   17

How VoIP Carries a Conversation   20

VoIP Features   22

Power in VoIP Networks   22

Putting It All Together   23

Chapter 3   Advantages of Broadband Phone Services   25

Lowering Your Monthly Phone Bill   25

Infrastructure Costs   25

Transport Costs   26

Regulatory Compliance   26

Taxes and Fees   26

Phone Number Flexibility   27

Keeping Your Same Phone Number   27

Virtual Phone Numbers   29

Online Call Management   31

Voice Mail   31

Call Forwarding   32

Call Logs   32

Click to Dial   32

Summary of Advantages   32

Chapter 4   Knowing Your Limits   33

Reliability   33

It's Electric   33

Reliance on Broadband and the Internet   34

Voice Quality   35
   911 and E911   37
   How 911 and E911 Works   37
   The Challenge for VoIP   39
Solutions   40
Summary of Limitations   43

Chapter 5   **From the Geek Squad Files   45**

Part II   **Choosing an Internet Phone Service   48**

Chapter 6   **Inventory of Broadband Phone Services   49**
Internet VoIP Phone Services   49
Cable VoIP Digital Phone Services   50
VoIP Chat Services   52
Summary of Broadband Phone Services   53

Chapter 7   **Selecting an Internet Phone Service   55**
What Will I Use It For?   55
   What Is My Backup Plan?   56
   Power   56
   Backup Line   57
Keeping a Minimal PSTN Line   57
   Which Service Should I Choose?   57
   Looking at Total Costs   57
   Is It Reliable Enough?   61
   Does It Have the Features You Need?   61
   Are Specialized Devices Supported?   61
   Revisiting Safety and 911   62
Comparing Plans   62
Summary   66

Chapter 8   **Selecting VoIP Equipment   67**
Cable VoIP Service Equipment   67
   Internet VoIP Service Equipment   68
   Choosing a Terminal Adapter   68
What Do the Internet VoIP Providers Offer?   71
VoIP Chat Service Equipment   72
Summary   72

Chapter 9   **From the Geek Squad Files   73**

Part III   **Going VoIP at Home   76**

Chapter 10   **Connecting the VoIP Equipment   77**
Starting Point   77
Connecting Cable VoIP Service   77
   Connecting Internet VoIP Service   79
   Signing Up for Service   79
   Installing a Stand-alone Terminal Adapter   80
   Installing an Integrated Router/Terminal Adapter   81

Connecting VoIP Chat Service   83

Making a Test Call   83

911 or E911 Registration   84

Summary   85

Addendum: Manually Configuring Terminal Adapters for Home Networks Using Static IP Addresses   85

Chapter 11   Making VoIP Accessible Throughout Your Home   87

Using Cordless Phones with VoIP   87

Separate PSTN and VoIP Lines   88

Two-Line Cordless Phones   89

Using Your Home Telephone Wiring with VoIP   90

Introduction to Home Telephone Wiring   90

Getting Access to Two Lines   92

Home Wiring with Cable VoIP Service   93

Home Wiring with Internet VoIP Service   95

Issues with Multiple Handsets   96

Overloading Your Terminal Adapter's Ringer Equivalence Number   96

Simultaneous Handsets Off Hook   97

Multiline VoIP Services   98

Specialized Phone Devices   100

Fax   101

TiVo and Satellite Receiver Boxes   101

Home Security/Alarm Systems   101

Summary   102

Chapter 12   Using Wireless Networks to Extend VoIP   103

Wireless Bridges   103

Wireless Phone Jacks   104

Summary   106

Chapter 13   Troubleshooting: Can You Hear Me Now?   107

Classify the Trouble   107

Service Connection Problems   107

Voice Quality Issues   110

Broadband Speed   110

Broadband Network Quality   112

Other Issues   115

Dialing-Related Issues   115

Getting Additional Help from Your VoIP Provider   115

Summary   116

Chapter 14   From the Geek Squad Files   117

Part IV   **VoIP Chat Services**   **120**

Chapter 15   **VoIP Chat Services**   **121**

Instant Messaging   121

     Client-Server   122

Peer-to-Peer   122

Internet Messaging with Voice   125

Summary   128

Chapter 16   **Using Skype and Google Talk**   **129**

Installing and Using Skype   129

     Improving Your Audio Quality   131

     Calling People Who Have "Real" Phones (and Phone Numbers)   133

Getting Calls from People Who Use "Real" Phones   134

     Installing and Using Google Talk   135

     Adding Contacts in Google Talk   137

Using Google Talk   138

Summary   138

Chapter 17   **The Future of Telephony**   **139**

A Review of What We Have Now   139

The Cost Battle: Consumers Versus Companies and Governments   139

System Convergence   140

     Future Use Scenario   140

     Mitigating Factor No. 1: Intrasystem Cooperation   143

Mitigating Factor No. 2: Battery Life and Size   144

Conclusion   144

Chapter 18   **From the Geek Squad Files**   **145**

Glossary   **147**

Index   **153**

Foreword

A couple of years ago I pondered what some considered to be an absurd idea: Why couldn't the backbone that serves up millions of page views a second carry voice too? And why couldn't we literally unplug the phone company and plug our phone into our Internet connection?

The idea didn't turn out to be as absurd as some thought, and based upon this concept, and a technology called voice over Internet Protocol (VoIP), Vonage was born in 2001. Using an existing high-speed Internet connection, Vonage technology enables anyone to make and receive phone calls, worldwide, with a touch-tone telephone—a feature-rich and cost effective alternative to traditional telephony services.

The most important concept to think about with VoIP and all its related applications is that VoIP has passed the early adopter stage, and has proven its durability, which makes us all ecstatic. VoIP is working not only for the technically gifted, but also for the average consumer. Today, more than 4 million U.S. households use VoIP.

Hence this timely book, *Internet Phone Services Simplified,* which addresses the exciting technologies behind broadband phone services and provides the reader with the information needed to make informed decisions about which phone service is right for them. The book starts with an overview of VoIP, followed by guidance on selecting a service. Also covered is how to take full advantage of some special features that broadband service providers offer, such as online call management and Vonage's virtual number service, as well as the best way to integrate phone services with your home network and telephones.

Internet Phone Services Simplified not only demonstrates the fantastic flexibility and feature-rich services enabled by VoIP, but it will also help you to understand your options in choosing a broadband service that is right for you. So, if you are ready to explore an exciting alternative to traditional phone service that will allow you to communicate in a more efficient, less costly manner, then this is the book for you.

Sincerely,

Jeffrey A. Citron

Vonage Chairman and Chief Strategist

Introduction

You have most likely heard about Internet telephony or voice over IP (also known as VoIP) by now (the terms are fairly interchangeable). It's free, it's great, it's everything the advertisements say it is, and it is applicable to everyone. Or is it?

This books examines Internet phone services in more detail, giving you what we hope is a clear picture of what they are and what they are not. You have many things to consider before subscribing to an Internet telephony service. This book walks you through all the considerations and separates the truth from the hype.

In addition to providing you with the information you need to determine whether VoIP is right for you, this book gives you a step-by-step walk-through of how to install it and integrate it with your existing home network and telephones. We also look into some more advanced Internet telephony options that are growing in popularity.

Starting Assumptions

We assume that you already have a home network installed and running in your home. We also assume that you have (or will acquire) high-speed broadband Internet service. We don't cover how to set up a home network in this book or how to get connected with high-speed broadband Internet service. If you need help with either, we recommend that you pick up a copy of our other book, *Home Networking Simplified.*

Microsoft Windows

For all PC setups used in this book, we reference only Microsoft Windows because it is the most common operating system in use today. If you are using a different operating system, the configurations, instructions, and screen shots may not directly apply, but the underlying principles and tasks are common across most operating systems in use today.

Mostly Linksys

As we did in *Home Networking Simplified,* we once again use Linksys equipment exclusively for our networking gear. We believe that Linksys has the most comprehensive and easy-to-use/install home networking product suite. In fact, the only time we stray from Linksys in this book is when the company doesn't make the type of device we are looking for (which is rare). One benefit of all this is device compatibility, which becomes important as the network you build (and the number of devices connected to it) grows.

Tips from the Geek Squad

At the end of each section of this book is a chapter written by our good friends from the Geek Squad. For those of you not familiar with the Geek Squad (http://www.geeksquad.com), it is a 24-hour computer support task force established to protect society from the assault of computerized technology. The Geek Squad saves your backside and protects you from the evil forces of inefficient networks, crashing hard drives, and corrupt files. It can do the following things:

- Restrain misbehaving hard drives and recover recalcitrant data
- Rehabilitate disobedient operating systems
- Make nonprinting printers print, nonscanning scanners scan, and nonconnecting connections connect
- Isolate, quarantine, and destroy computer/software viruses
- Resuscitate dead laptops, PDAs, and desktops
- End unruly computer activity, reestablishing humanity's dominance over technology
- Secure networks from intruders, keeping them buttoned down and for your eyes only
- Allow you to throw away every manual you never were going to read anyway

In short, if you ever have a computer or network problem, call the Geek Squad.

These fine folks have agreed to help us help you. With you in mind, they have agreed to read, review, and debug our notes and design plans. The chapters that the Geek Squad provides are a collection of notes, lessons learned, and anecdotes that this unique computer support company has collected over the years while helping home networking users with computer and network problems. In addition, you see tips from the Geek Squad interspersed throughout the book when a common issue or important point warrants a separate callout. We flag these tips with a Geek Squad icon.

PART **I**

PART I
Internet Telephony Fundamentals

To start the book off, we thought it would be a good idea to walk you through the benefits and trade-offs of using an Internet-based telephone system, sometimes referred to as *Voice over IP (VoIP)*, or broadband phone service.

To understand the benefits at a deeper level, we begin this section with a short primer on the public telephone system that you have probably used your entire life. There's nothing too technical here, just a quick look into the simple, yet well-designed communication system that has been in operation for nearly 100 years.

We follow Chapter 1, "Traditional Phone Systems," with a similar type of primer for the new VoIP system that is the focus of this book. How does it work, why is it different, and how reliable is it? We answer questions you have had or possibly still do. Again, it's not overly technical, just what you need to know so that it doesn't all seem like voodoo and black magic.

After we have the basics down on how the two systems work, we can present a complete picture of the benefits and features, as well as the trade-offs between the two systems. We believe that VoIP offers some substantial advantages, but they need to be discussed in light of the current limitations of the technology.

Despite what many commercials claim, using VoIP has some limitations, particularly if you choose to completely replace your standard phone line. In some cases, this is a good choice, but in other cases, it might not be. If you take the time to inform yourself with a book such as this, you will hopefully be much happier with your decision.

When used properly, Internet phone services can offer significant advantages. As we said earlier, our aim for this book is to enable our readers to make good choices based on relevant information. Our reliance on the phone system and voice communications in our daily lives requires nothing less.

CHAPTER 1

Traditional Phone Systems

Before we get into broadband phone services, it is helpful to spend a few minutes understanding the traditional telephone system, known as the public switched telephone network (PSTN). The public telephone system has been in place in some parts of the world for over 100 years and has remained relatively unchanged in principle over most of its existence. Remarkably, even though the underlying technology has evolved several times, the same telephones that your parents or grandparents had when they grew up still work with the phone system today.

It's easy to overlook how amazing and reliable the public telephone system is. When you pick up a phone, you expect to hear a dial tone, much the same way that you expect there to be air when you breathe. How many other man-made systems have you come to rely on and expect to work every time, all the time? Probably not too many. What's even more impressive is that if you have access to a phone connection anywhere in the world, you can reach any other phone in the world, and in some cases, you don't even need to know the other phone's number. Consider also that this has now been possible for several decades. The achievement is staggering. In fact, the creation of the phone system had a tremendous economic, social, and political impact, as it was the first worldwide communication system accessible from the home.

The real beauty is the elegant simplicity of the design: two wires, a speaker, and a microphone. That's all that is required to talk to someone on the other side of the planet. Well, at least that's all you need in your house. Beyond your house, a lot is going on. That's where things get interesting, and we spend the rest of the chapter talking about it. While we think it is interesting just from a technology standpoint, the information about how the "old" system works can help you make better choices about if and when to switch to the new system.

In the Beginning

When telephone systems were first deployed, every phone was physically hard-wired to the local switchboard, which was monitored full- or part-time by a live operator. When a person picked up the handset (as shown in the following figure), the switchboard sensed the change on that circuit, and a bell or a light at the switchboard would alert the operator that you wanted to place a call. The operator would then ask you who you wanted to speak with. At that point, she would ring the phone of the person you wanted to speak with and tell the person you were on the line. She would then place a jumper cable between the end of your circuit and the end of the other caller's circuit, thus completing the connection between the two callers.

Operator-Based Telephone Network

Back then, phone numbers did not exist, and the local operator just asked for the other party's name, which was labeled on the switchboard. In cases where a person needed to speak with someone in another town, the operator would ring the circuit connecting her switchboard to the switchboard of the other town, or the next switchboard in the line. With each switchboard, a new operator was needed to complete the call. Regardless of the number of switches you had to go through, however, the operators performed the same function, namely, completing an electric circuit between two phones so that people could talk to each other.

For the first several years of its existence, this is how the phone system worked, and it worked just fine. As the popularity grew, one problem that developed was that more people wanted to place calls, and they wanted to talk to people farther away. This overloaded operators when they tried to keep up with all the call traffic.

Rise of the Machines

As in most cases with technology, solving one problem often leads to another one somewhere else, at least temporarily. In this case, the problem with replacing manual operators with something more automated was simply, "How can a machine know what a person means when he says he wants to talk to Aunt Gertrude who lives in Selma?" The answer, of course, was the invention of the telephone number.

Invented by the engineering gods at AT&T Bell Labs in 1947 (and we mean that with all due respect—it seems that those people invented just about everything that has to do with telecommunications), the numbering system allowed rapid expansion of an automated, scalable, and worldwide telephone system. The numbering system devised and eventually adopted is referred to as the *3-3-4 system*.

 Note At least one other system was in use before the current 3-3-4 system that you are most familiar with. One of the first versions used a one- or two-letter exchange name abbreviation along with two to five digits—such as B-6463 or PE6-5000. As far as we can tell, the first use of the 3-3-4 system was in Wichita Falls, Texas, in 1958, nearly 11 years after the first telephone number was invented.

The logic behind the 3-3-4 system is that it not only solved the problem of how to route phone calls, but the segmentation also made it easy for most people to remember their phone number and several others. It's worth reviewing how the system works because of some recent changes in telephone regulations.

In the United States, the telephone numbers were assigned in blocks as follows:

(XXX)	XXX-	XXXX
Area Code	**Exchange Prefix**	**Line Number**

To follow the logic of the design, we discuss the number blocks out of order:

- **Exchange prefix**—The prefix corresponds to the mechanical switch, also known as a central office (CO), that sent our original operators to the unemployment line. Think of a CO as serving a particular town. A larger city might have several COs.

  From the day the system was invented until about 2000, every phone number was physically tied to a specific CO. This meant that if you moved, you had to get a new phone number.

Local Number Portability (LNP) is now available in most locations and from most providers. This is discussed in Chapter 3, "Advantages of Broadband Phone Services," but in a nutshell, phone numbers are no longer tied to a physical phone line.

- **Line number**—This is the number that is assigned to your phone line (but not necessarily to a single phone handset). Because the number is tied to the line and not the handset, you can easily switch phone handsets. Without this cool feature, the princess phone would never have been invented, without which the lives of our technical reviewers would have been a little less complete.

- **Area code**—The use of the area code is what makes the entire system scalable. Think of an area code as identifying a particular region or collection of cities. The cool thing is that it allows for both new population centers to spring up and for the number of users in an existing area to grow without much trouble.

Each area code provides about 8 million usable numbers out of a possible 10 million combinations. Those 2 million or so numbers are unusable because of things such as 911, 411, and all the seven-digit numbers that are unavailable because they start with a 1 or 0, as well as toll and toll-free numbers such as 900 and 800 numbers.

The system described in the preceding list is oriented to the United States. To make an international call, dialing 0-1-1 gets you the international exchange (from the United States). Countries outside the United States often have different numbering schemes, some of which include city codes. Line numbers can also be longer than four digits.

With the addition of phone numbers and mechanical switches, a phone call was made by dialing the phone number of the person you were calling. Originally the dialing was done using a rotary dial that made a series of clicks on the phone line: one click for a 1, two clicks for a 2, and so on. The mechanical switch listened to the clicks and could automatically connect the call to the dialed number.

During the 1970s and 1980s, the mechanical switches in the telephone system were replaced with digital switches. Digital switches are essentially powerful computers that can connect thousands of calls automatically. To the person at home, only small changes were made to the way that phone calls

Electronically Switched Telephone Network

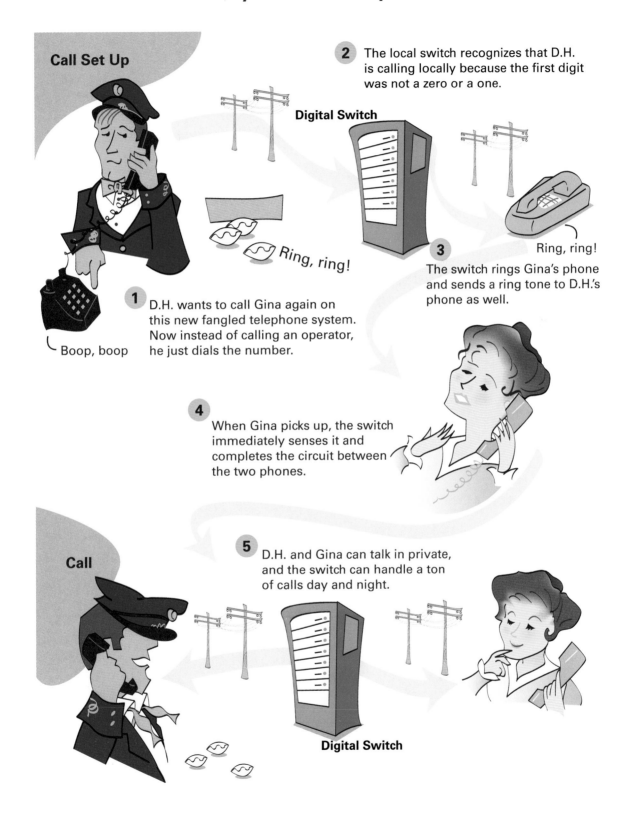

were placed. One change was that instead of dialing numbers on a rotary dial, keypads appeared on handsets and "tone" dialing replaced rotary dialing. When you push a button on the phone, an audio tone is created (called dual-tone multifrequency [DTMF]). The digital switch "hears" the tones on your line and interprets how to route your call.

So far, everything we have talked about revolves around calling the person across the street, also connected to the same CO, or switch, that you are. What about calling someone in another city?

Ma Bell

Hopefully we still have your attention. Stick with us just a couple of pages longer, and we promise you will understand why we need to talk about this stuff.

Prior to 1984, the Bell System was pretty much one big company that handled all the phone subscribers and the calls they made. The United States is a very large area, with many cities. How do you interconnect them all? One way would be for each city to have a line to every other city. This would be costly and rather a mess. So the phone system was designed in a hierarchical fashion (see Figure 1-1, intentionally oversimplified).

Figure 1-1   Hierarchical Telephone Network Design

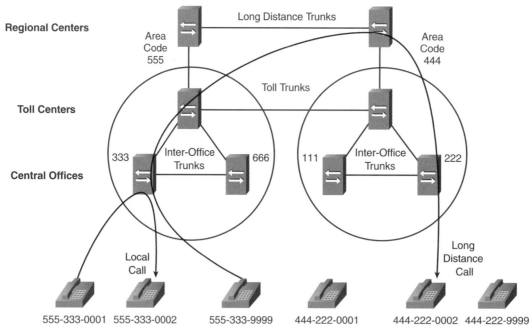

Central offices made up the bottom of the tree and connected the lines from homes and businesses to the telephone network. These switches were connected to other switches in the same general geographic area, for example, nearby cities, using trunks. A *trunk* is just a fancy term for a set of wires between switches that can carry a bunch of calls. Calls to other people in the same town were generally completed by the local CO, or perhaps between two COs. Commonly, calls connected using only the bottom level of the tree are included in a flat-rate service, meaning that you pay one monthly price for any number of calls.

Toll centers make up the middle tier. When a call was to be connected between two more-distant COs, the call was passed up the tree to a toll switch. Toll switches connect to other toll switches (using toll trunks), which in turn connect to COs in other geographic areas. For example, a call between Dallas, Texas, and Fort Worth, Texas, might have passed through toll switches. Toll calls, as the name implies, typically incur a fee in addition to your monthly flat-rate service.

The top of the tree are regional centers. When a call was to be connected between two COs in two different geographic regions, for example, using two different area codes (not always true, but it makes a good example), the call was passed up by the COs to the toll centers, then passed up again to the regional centers, who would route the call to the appropriate other regional center, and then back down the tree. Typically these were billed as long-distance calls.

 Note We are intentionally oversimplifying the hierarchy, which in reality had five tiers, or classes, of switches. Three levels are fine for this discussion.

The system worked fantastically, outages were fairly rare, and for some 30 years, everyone was happy. Well, not everyone. There was the little matter of the phone company's monopoly to deal with. Because phone lines were physically tied to a single telephone switch that belonged to a single telephone company, as a consumer you had little choice as to your phone service or the rates you would pay.

Breaking Up the Happy Family

Enter Judge Green. In 1984, the Bell System was essentially declared a monopoly and broken into smaller companies. Seven regional Bell operating companies (RBOCs) were created to provide local and regional phone services. AT&T was relegated to providing long-distance services between RBOCs (see Figure 1-2).

Figure 1-2   1984 Divestiture Companies

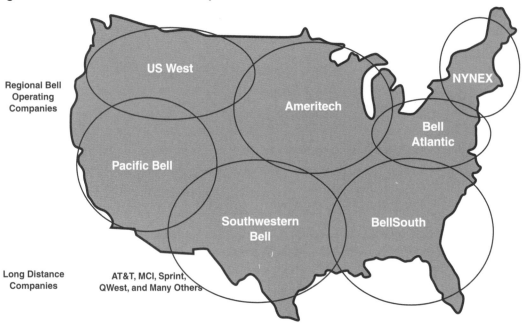

Under the "equal access" provision of the judgment, other companies were also invited to provide long-distance services, and the RBOCs were told to cooperate. A flurry of new companies was born, including MCI, Sprint, Qwest, and others. RBOCs were prohibited from offering long-distance, and long-distance providers were similarly prohibited from offering local phone services. Arguably, the result of this shake-up of the phone system was increased competition and lower overall phone service rates to consumers, particularly for long-distance calls. Consumers could now choose their long-distance provider, and the slamming wars began.

 Slamming is when your long-distance company uses measures not quite on the up-and-up to obtain your long-distance business. In many cases, a subscriber's long-distance company was simply changed without her consent. In other cases, the subscriber was not fully aware that the telemarketing pitch she was getting was going to result in a change to her long-distance provider. Slamming is now a Federal Communications Commission (FCC) violation. Check out http://www.fcc.gov/slamming/ if you feel that you might have been a victim of such practices.

You must understand two important points about this turning point in telecommunications. First, it was successful at opening the phone system to competition, albeit only the long-distance services initially. Local phone services still had a huge challenge—how do you have competition when only a single set of wires are physically connected to a home or business? The RBOCs made the investment to install all the wiring. Should they then be forced to turn these assets over to other companies? Aside from ownership and investments, there was also the matter of logistics of having multiple companies burying or stringing numerous sets of wires everywhere. So for now, local phone services still had little or no competition.

The second point to understand is that the breakup of the phone company caused dramatic changes in the way the phone system was architected. With no single centralized phone company, telecom companies had to change the way that their switches communicated with one another. Instead of relying on "higher-order" switches to make decisions on call routing, "lower-order" switches had to have more capability to communicate directly to other lower-order switches.

How would the FCC open the apparent stranglehold that the local phone companies had on the phone line?

Mobile Telephone System

Almost in parallel, starting about 1982, mobile phones got their start in the marketplace. The FCC granted two licenses (known as the A and B blocks) in each market to operate mobile phone systems. The RBOCs, rich with cash, quickly gobbled up a license in each market; however, they were prohibited from monopolizing through a stipulation that the other license in each market had to be allocated to a non-RBOC company (initially long-distance providers were also prohibited).

Companies such as Cellular One sprung up and began to offer mobile phone services in competition with the RBOCs. This was perhaps the first credible competition for local phone services, even though at the time, mobile phone services were perceived as a luxury for use in your car, not really at home. With handsets the size and weight of a brick, the word *luxury* was kind of a stretch.

But over the next few years, cellular phones went digital, as did the mobile systems themselves. By 1995, there were approximately 25 million wireless subscribers, compared with roughly 160 million wired phone subscribers. Just a year earlier, the FCC began allocating up to six additional licenses (known as the PCS A, B, C, D, E, and F blocks) in each market, again with restrictions on the RBOCs, but this time allowing the long-distance providers to throw their hats into the ring. AT&T lunged at the opportunity (AT&T Wireless) as did Sprint (Sprint PCS), while the others curiously sat on the sidelines.

The wireless phone system was built to be interconnected with the wired phone system so that calls can be connected back and forth between them. Wireless systems generally have the same kinds of elements as wired systems—switches, handsets, and gateways to other systems such as the PSTN (see Figure 1-3).

Figure 1-3   Modern Digital Telephone Network Design

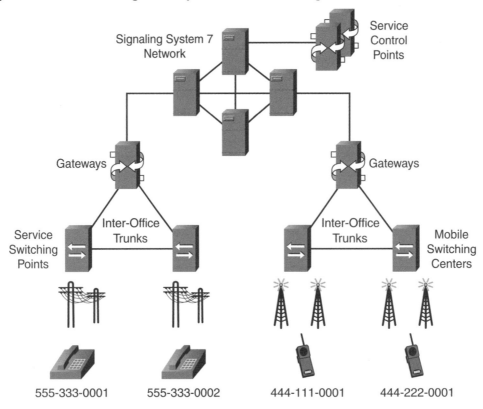

 Note Again, we are intentionally oversimplifying the network structure. We have reduced it to just a few essentials for the sake of discussion.

In the current global telephone system, wired and wireless phones are connected to either service switching points (SSPs) or mobile switching centers (MSCs). Calls are set up between any two places in the network (whether it's a wired-to-wired call, wired-to-wireless call, and so on) by sending digital messages to each other through a common network called the Signaling System 7 (SS7) network. Think of SS7 as a really smart coordinator that helps callers find each other.

Another important element of the SS7 network is the concept of a Service Control Point (SCP). SCPs enable services such as 800 numbers. When you dial an 800 number, lookups are done by an SCP to translate the 800 number to an actual number so that the call can be routed. SCPs also enable newer required services such as LNP.

In some countries, special area codes are assigned for mobile phones that are distinct from wired phones. In the United States, virtually no distinction exists when numbers are assigned.

For some time, massive competition existed for wireless phone services, with up to a half-dozen or more providers in some markets. Wireless phone services often offered free long-distance calls and were sometimes a reasonable substitute for having a wired phone. There are 600 to 800 million wireless phones sold worldwide each year.

Internet

About the same time the wireless phone system was exploding, the need for high-speed computer data services also exploded, leading to the expansion of the Internet.

Interestingly, the first access to the Internet for most homes was through the public telephone system, using dialup access to Internet services such as AOL and Earthlink.

More recently, high-speed broadband services are the primary access to the Internet. Although several types of access exist, the most popular by far are digital subscriber line (DSL) and cable. DSL is typically provided by your phone company using the same wires as your telephone service. Broadband cable service is typically offered by your television cable company using the same wires as your TV cable.

Consolidate, Merge, and Acquire

Four massive communications systems now existed: wired phones, wireless phones, the Internet, and cable TV; however, restrictions still existed on which companies could offer local services, long-distance services, and so on. Then came the Telecommunications Act of 1996, which removed restrictions and (quoted from the FCC) "let any communications business compete in any market against any other."

In the years after this sweeping regulatory change, massive consolidation occurred in the telecom industry. With most restrictions removed, mergers went wild. Qwest bought US West. SBC gobbled up Ameritech, PacBell, and AT&T (long-distance), and then dropped the SBC name in favor of the AT&T brand name. Voicestream bought a host of smaller wireless providers. Verizon was formed by a merger of Bell Atlantic and NYNEX. Sprint PCS gobbled up Nextel. Cingular swallowed AT&T Wireless. And so it continues today.

Where we had four or five separate smaller companies offering distinct services in each market, we now have four or five massive companies offering a suite of services in those markets. Take Verizon, for example, which can offer you local phone, long-distance, DSL, and wireless phone service.

The last frontier (or at least the next one) is the ensuing battle between cable TV providers and these massive service providers. Companies like Verizon, AT&T, and others will almost certainly be offering digital TV services soon. Cable TV providers are already launching headfirst into providing phone services to complement their broadband Internet services. In addition, numerous new players have emerged who offer VoIP services, including Vonage and others.

The conclusions that we can draw so far from all the activity in the telecom industry since 1984 are as follows:

- Competition was created and is (so far) alive and well.
- The services themselves have gotten cheaper for consumers.
- Subscribers have numerous and robust choices of service.

Important Things to Know About the PSTN

This really leads us to the rest of this book. The table is now set for one of the latest entrants to the telecom foray—broadband phone services. We spend the rest of this book explaining what they are and how they work, and we help you decide which one is right for you.

Before we continue, here is a short summary of critical points to remember about the public telephone system:

- **Power**—The power for a phone connected to the public telephone system is provided by the central office. This is why your phone still works even when your home electricity is out. As long as the central office has power, you have phone service.

- **Reliability**—The public telephone system is one of the most stable and reliable systems in the world. It is engineered for and regularly achieves (on average) 99.999 percent uptime (commonly referred to as the *five 9's standard*). Incidentally, of the 0.001 percent downtime, half of the failures are attributed to human errors, not the system itself. It's quite remarkable.

- **911 and E911**—Because of the reliability of the system and the ability to pinpoint the location of the caller, 911 services heavily depend on the public telephone system. As we discuss later, wireless phone services and broadband phone services still have some catching up to do in this area.

- **Number portability**—Previously in the public telephone system, numbers were tied to specific locations and lines. With LNP, you can now take your number with you, at least within a local geographic area. We discuss this more in later chapters.

- **Costs**—Because of the competition in long-distance and now local phone services, costs have come way down. It is now possible to get flat-rate unlimited public telephone services (in the United States) for $40–$50 per month, including unlimited calling and no long-distance charges.

- **Choices**—You as a consumer now have many choices for your telephone services. If you take away one thing from this book, it is to not accept the status quo of your current services and to take a new look at how you and your family use voice communications.

We now move on to take a look at one of those choices: broadband phone services, using Voice over IP (VoIP).

CHAPTER 2

Voice over IP (VoIP)

The term *Voice over IP (VoIP)* does not refer to a single service but encompasses an entire collection of services that can fill the phone service needs of many different residential and business customers. VoIP can be used by a service provider to optimize its capability to carry many calls. VoIP can be used by small and large businesses for their office phone systems. VoIP can also be used as a good alternative (or supplement) to the public phone system for residential phone service, which is the focus of this book.

You might already be using VoIP and not even know or realize it. Many telephone service providers are starting to use some form of VoIP (transparently to you) inside their networks because of the cost efficiencies it can afford them. Many online voice chat services, such as Xbox Live voice chat, Skype, and so on, rely on VoIP. You might find it worthwhile to spend a few minutes to understand how VoIP works. Don't worry, you don't need to know how it works to use it, but it might help to understand the advantages and limitations we discuss later.

Circuit Switching and Packet Switching

The main difference between traditional phone systems and VoIP systems is *circuit switching* versus *packet switching*. The public switched telephone network (PSTN) uses circuit switching to carry your voice from your phone to the person you are calling (see Figure 2-1). This means that while you are on the phone, a connection is made end-to-end through the phone system. This requires resources (in this case, a series of wires, switches, and connections) in the phone network that are dedicated for the duration of your call. While you are using them, no one else can use them. The end-to-end circuit is reserved for your conversation.

This approach works well, but imagine the resources that are required to carry millions of calls each day coast to coast. At first, each call required a separate set of copper wires. Technology got better, and now millions of calls can be carried over fiber-optic cables (and still circuits get overloaded on Mother's Day). But even though density improved, the basic principles of circuit switching still apply today—each call consumes a *channel* on the wire end to end for the duration of the call.

Figure 2-1   Circuit Switching Versus Packet Switching

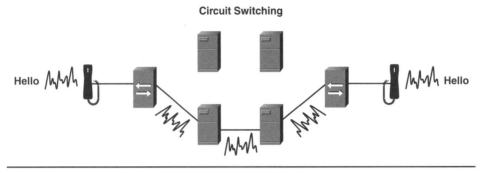

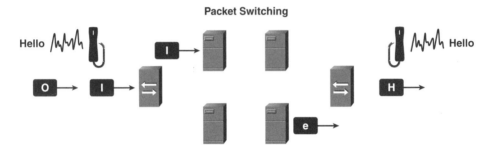

 Transoceanic fiber cables can carry more than 100 million phone calls each. Even the more ordinary fiber cables have thousands of strands but can carry 1 million+ calls.

Packet switching works differently (see Figure 2-1). Instead of having a dedicated connection end-to-end, packet switching breaks the voice conversation into pieces, transmits the pieces, and then reassembles the pieces at the other side back into the voice conversation. You might be asking yourself: How does that save anything? Well, if you remember in circuit switching, you are consuming a dedicated resource end-to-end. But in packet switching, many people can share that same resource at the same time.

In the example shown in Figure 2-1, the word *Hello* spoken by the caller is broken into five packets, one per letter sound, and transmitted across the network with millions of other packets from other phone conversations. The receiving switch or phone knows how to reassemble these five packets into the sounds spoken by the caller, and the word *Hello* is played out the handset speaker.

> **Note** Alas, we are intentionally oversimplifying again. In reality, it takes about 50 packets to transmit each second of speech. But we had a hard time finding a word in the dictionary with 50 letters that could be spoken within one second for use in our example.

The important difference to understand is that during a traditional phone call, you are using a dedicated circuit for the duration of your call. Transmission is constant. In packet switching, the pieces of the conversation find their own way through the network and are re-assembled on the other end, which allows many more conversation to take place than in curcuit switching. So, lots of other folks can use the same circuit at the same time you are.

How VoIP Works

Now that you understand a fundamental difference in the way VoIP compares to the PSTN, we look in more detail at how VoIP works. Any phone service has the following four primary components:

- **Signaling**—Refers to the communications between your handset and the phone service, for example, how the system recognizes you want to make a call, how it receives the number you want to call, and so on.

- **Conversation**—Sometimes referred to as the "bearer" component. This is the actual voice conversation being transmitted and received across the network.

- **Features**—Phone services offer many features including call waiting, call forwarding, voice mail, and so on.

- **Power**—How the handset in your home receives electric power for it to operate.

VoIP Signaling

Signaling refers to how a central office switch in the phone network communicates between itself and your phone, or to other switches in the network. You need to understand a few important signals.

First, how does the phone network know you want to place a call? As Figure 2-2 illustrates, when you lift the handset in your house, this signals the phone network that you want to make a call. You might not realize it, but when you lift the handset, the first thing the central office does is send you a dial tone sound. Then you happily dial your numbers, which is the next step in signaling. After you have dialed, the phone network sends and receives a flurry of digital messages across the rest of the phone system to determine how to route your call. The destination central office then notifies the person you are calling by ringing his handset.

Figure 2-2   PSTN-to-PSTN Call (No VoIP)

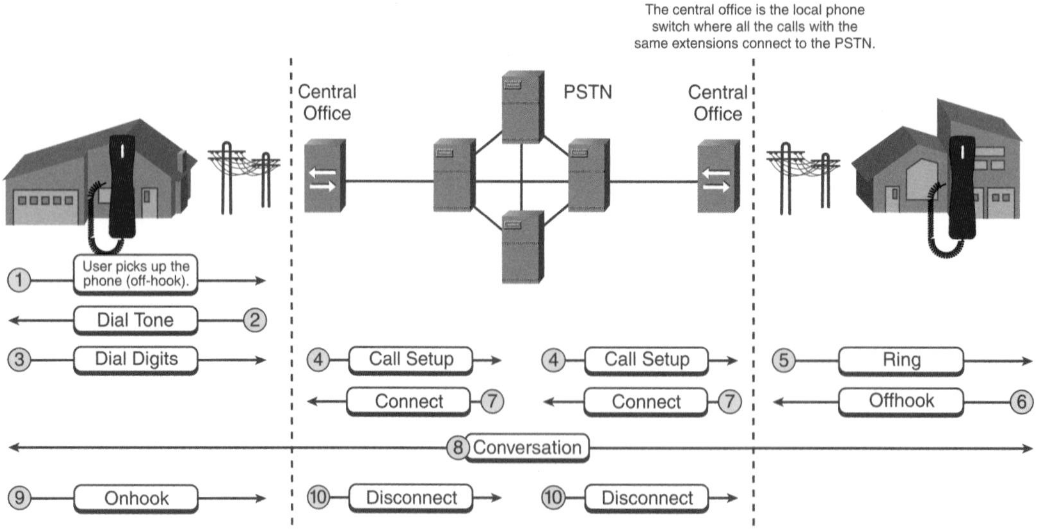

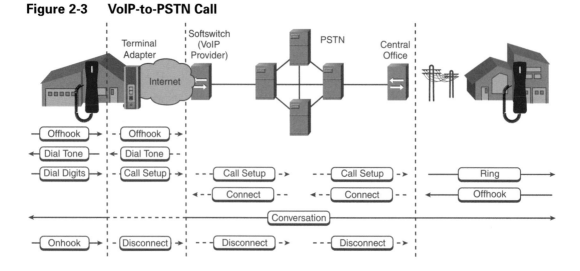

If the person you called answers, a conversation path is set up between you and the person you called for the duration of the call. When one of you hangs up, the central office is signaled to disconnect the call. Again, after some magic digital messages inside the phone network, the call is disconnected. An important thing to understand is that in the case of a call between two traditional phones on the PSTN, the part inside your house works pretty much the same way (analog) that it worked 20 or 30 years ago.

We now look at how this changes if the caller is using a broadband phone service (that is, VoIP) and calls the same person with a PSTN phone service, as shown in Figure 2-3.

Figure 2-3   VoIP-to-PSTN Call

In this case, a terminal adapter now connects the handset in your house to your broadband Internet connection. The terminal adapter acts as a translator, converting the handset signals into VoIP signals (in other words, it takes the analog voice and converts it to a digital signal). For example, when you lift the handset, instead of the central office recognizing that your phone is off hook, the terminal adapter translates it to a message sent to the broadband phone provider that you want to place a call.

From that point, the signaling is similar to the PSTN example previously described, except at each step, the terminal adapter is translating your phone handset actions into digital messages that are being sent over your broadband Internet connection to the broadband phone service provider's softswitch. The softswitch takes care of routing your call, just like the central office would. Notice that in this case, the call is still routed through the PSTN to the person you are calling. This is done by a gateway between the broadband phone service and the PSTN. To you, it's totally transparent.

Note *Softswitch* refers to a central office switch, except instead of having a bunch of phone lines connected to it, it only receives digital messages. The "soft" part refers to the fact that it's a telephone switch without hard wires connected to it. While a central office needs to be in fairly close proximity to you, a softswitch could be thousands of miles away—anywhere the messages can reach it. Think of a softswitch as a fast computer that understands how to route telephone calls.

Finally, we take a look at how this changes if both the caller and the called party are using broadband phone services (not necessarily even the same one), as shown in Figure 2-4.

Figure 2-4   VoIP-to-VoIP Call (No PSTN)

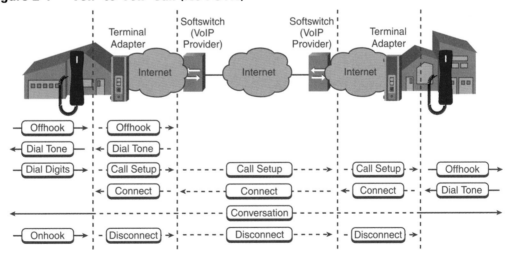

In this case, a terminal adapter now connects both handsets to their broadband Internet connections. The caller goes off hook and dials the destination number. The softswitch that serves the caller routes the call to the softswitch that serves the called number. The destination terminal adapter gets a digital message for the incoming call and converts it to ring the handset.

When the called person picks up the phone, again a flurry of digital messages are exchanged between terminal adapters and softswitches on both ends, and voilà, the call is connected.

Another important function to understand about the terminal adapter is that it converts your voice conversation into packets that can be sent over the Internet. The next section discusses how this is possible.

How VoIP Carries a Conversation

Human speech is made up of analog sound waves, which can be transmitted using straightforward techniques. A phone on the PSTN can represent your voice as a continuous stream of voltage changes on a copper wire (this is referred to as a *carrier signal*). When the carrier signal reaches the other end (the receiving phone), the electric signals excite a diaphragm (more commonly known as a speaker), which produces a good approximation, or "analogy," of your voice.

For digital telephony (including VoIP), a dedicated circuit does not transmit the voice, so human speech must be converted to a digital stream (or a series of 1s and 0s) by the transmitter and then re-created on the receiving end. Analog-to-digital conversion is accomplished by sampling, which is the process of taking many instantaneous measurements of an analog signal.

If you were to look at human speech on a meter, it would look something like what Figure 2-5 illustrates.

Figure 2-5   Analog Waveform of Human Speech

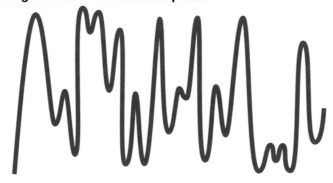

To convert this waveform into a digital signal, the waveform is measured thousands of times per second. For every voltage level (which is what you are measuring), a corresponding combination of 1s and 0s exists, and that combination is sent across the digital network. This process of measuring and converting is called *sampling*. On the receiving end, the combination of 1s and 0s is read and the corresponding voltage is re-created.

If enough samples are taken, the original analog signal can be nearly exactly replicated by "connecting the dots" of the instantaneous measurements re-created on the receiving end (see Figure 2-6).

Figure 2-6   Packetizing Voice

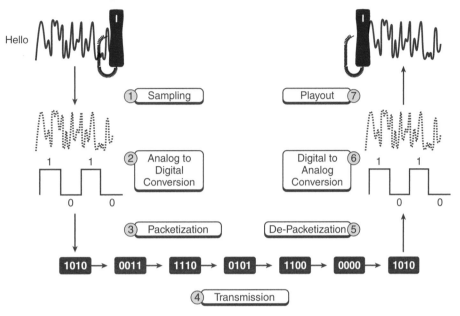

The trick for "near exact" replication of the original signal is to take the right amount of samples, because too few samples can result in multiple waveforms that could *possibly* connect the dots (and remember, we are trying to *exactly* match the waveform). Too many samples can provide fantastic sound quality, but it can also require too much data transmission to be cost effective. The right amount turns out to be twice the rate of the highest frequency in the waveform. For the sake of simplicity, consider a pure tone of 1000 Hz. Figure 2-7 illustrates what the tone would look like on a meter.

Figure 2-7   Waveform of a Pure, 1000-Hz Tone

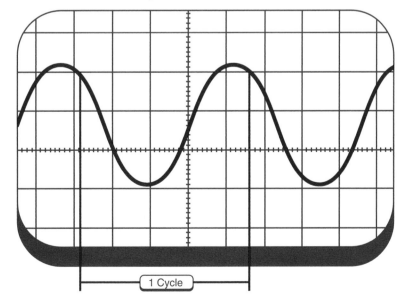

Hertz (Hz) is also referred to as cycles per second, and in this case, the pattern or cycle on the scope would repeat 1000 times per second. This signal can be nearly perfectly replicated going from analog (the tone) to digital and then back to analog by measuring the signal 2000 times per second. This rate (the rate required for good replication) is called the *Nyquist rate,* named after the clever fellow who figured it out.

Human speech is a jumble of many different tones, ranging from very low (bass) sounds of 100 Hz up to treble sounds of about 1700 Hz and higher. With harmonics and other "noises," speech includes tones of up to about 4000 Hz. Therefore, to replicate all the sounds, speech is usually sampled at about 8000 times per second.

 What did they say? OK, sampling is a bit complicated. Think of it like this. If you wanted to paint a picture of a flower, you would probably look at the flower, paint a little, look at the flower again, paint a little, and so on until you completed the painting. Speech sampling is similar. The VoIP phone "looks at" your voice about 8000 times per second while it is preparing the information to transmit to the other phone about what sounds you are making.

After enough samples are taken, the data (in the form of bytes) is shoved into a packet and sent on its way to the other phone (see Figure 2-6). When the packet reaches the other phone, the sampled data re-creates the original waveform, which excites a diaphragm, which moves a speaker, producing your grandma's voice from the old country telling you about this year's bumper beet crop.

VoIP Features

With your traditional phone service, you have no doubt become accustomed to a bunch of features such as call waiting, call forwarding, caller ID, and so on. How do these change with a broadband phone service?

Simple—they don't. You still get the features you are used to as well as a few new cool ones that we talk about in the next chapter. The features work similarly to those you have become used to with the PSTN.

Power in VoIP Networks

You might be asking yourself why you need to know where a broadband phone gets its electric power. It's an important issue to understand.

With the public telephone system, your phone receives its power from the central office switch (see Figure 2-8). This means that even when your home has no power, your phone still does, as long as the central office itself has power. The same set of wires that carry your voice conversation also send power to your handset.

Figure 2-8   Where Does My Phone Get Its Power From?

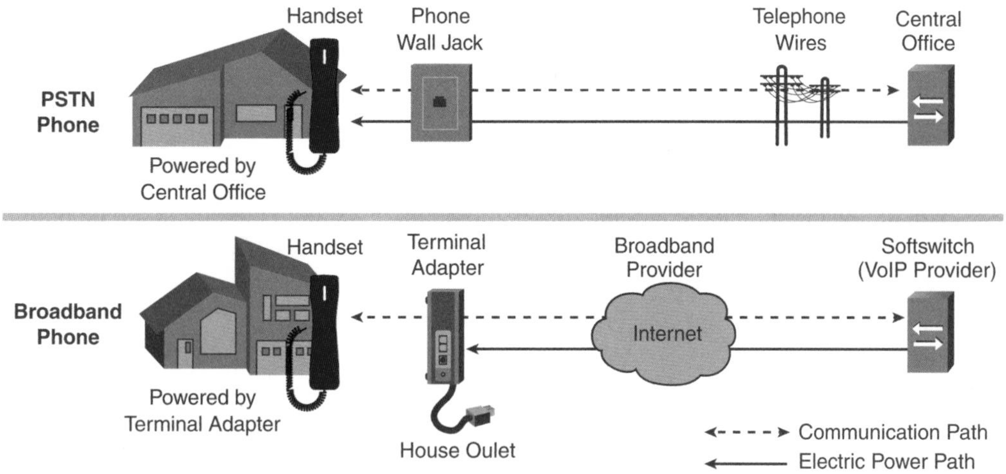

Handset   Phone
Wall Jack

Telephone
Wires

Central
Office

PSTN
Phone

Powered by
Central Office

Handset   Terminal
Adapter

Broadband
Provider

Softswitch
(VoIP Provider)

Broadband
Phone

Internet

Powered by
Terminal Adapter

House Oulet

◄ - - - - ► Communication Path
◄─────── Electric Power Path

In the case of a broadband phone service, electric powering is different. The broadband connection between your house and your broadband provider does not provide power, only a data communication path. In this case, the terminal adapter itself provides the power to your handset. Terminal adapters are plugged into the electric outlet in your house; therefore, if your house loses electricity, so does the terminal adapter, and more importantly, so does the handset.

Chapter 4, "Knowing Your Limits," covers some of the limitations with broadband phone services, such as loss of electricity, in more depth.

Many people routinely ditch their trusty old telephone handsets for new-fangled cordless phones. Interestingly enough, these phones require electricity in your house to power the base. This is why when you lose electricity, your cordless phone typically does not work. Most people haven't really thought about it, but if you are concerned, you should always keep one traditional handset plugged into a telephone use VoIP).

Putting It All Together

We've just looked at how broadband phone service works in comparison to traditional telephone service. As you can see, a lot of similarities and a few important distinctions exist.

In general, how you use your handset to place and receive calls does not change. Even the handsets you now have in your home can still be used.

What does change is how your call is handled inside the network and how your voice is carried. Other than that, the providers have done a great job of integrating into the public telephone system to make it nearly painless to consumers.

So that is what you need to know about the network and the technology for both the traditional phone network and the VoIP network. With this knowledge, we can now discuss the advantages and limitations of broadband phone services.

CHAPTER 3

Advantages of Broadband Phone Services

Why are so many people subscribing to broadband phone services, either as an additional phone line or as a complete replacement to their traditional phone service? The primary reason is cost. But as you will see, other advantages exist as well.

Lowering Your Monthly Phone Bill

What attracted most people to Voice over IP (VoIP), even when the quality was still questionable, was the fact that you could make free and unlimited long-distance calls. Now that the quality is good, and the calls are still relatively inexpensive, so much the better. How low is low? We examine different service plans available in Chapter 7, "Selecting an Internet Phone Service." The bottom line is, you can get a broadband phone service with unlimited calling and no nationwide long-distance charges (international calls do cost extra) for $25–30 a month.

How can broadband companies offer phone services more cheaply than the traditional phone companies? The following four primary factors make broadband phone services so inexpensive:

- Infrastructure costs

- Transport costs

- Regulatory compliance costs

- Taxes and fees

Infrastructure Costs

First and foremost, the costs for the public telephone infrastructure—that is, the central offices, long-distance switches, transport lines, and wiring into every home and business across the globe—are immensely expensive investments. Tens of billions of dollars are spent each year just to upgrade, expand, and maintain this network.

In contrast, broadband phone services do not have similar infrastructure costs. Instead, these services are made possible by strategically located VoIP gateways (which translate between VoIP and public switched telephone network [PSTN] systems) throughout the geographic areas they are serving. Beyond that, you are using your Internet connection, so you have no additional wiring costs. Keep in mind that we are referring to the telephone provider's cost, which is passed on to consumers.

VoIP, on the other hand, uses a data network that was a much less expensive network to set up and maintain. If that wasn't a good enough deal, the section of the network that is the most expensive (the part that goes from the local office to your house) is owned (and therefore maintained) by the phone or cable companies. Because the network treats voice the same way that it treats data (with unlimited uploading and downloading for a monthly fee), you can get unlimited long-distance for a great price.

Transport Costs

Similar to infrastructure costs, public telephone services incur certain costs when a telephone call must be carried long distances to more-distant central offices.

By their nature, broadband phone services use the public Internet as the primary transport. Because the conversion of your voice into packets works just like the packets that carry e-mail, it's easy to see why no additional cost is incurred with a call from one VoIP phone to another. To the Internet, a packet is a packet is a packet. The Internet service provider (ISP) simply charges you a monthly fee (in most countries) for the Internet connection and you talk away. This structure does fall apart though if the network runs out of capacity someday, because the ISPs would have to spend money to upgrade their networks. With the relatively low bandwidth required for VoIP calls, capacity is not really an issue today, but if Internet videophones take off, you could see costs go up.

The real trick to making VoIP worth a darn, however, is that the calls are still cheap when calling PSTN phones anywhere in the country, and in some cases even international calls are relatively cheap. With the strategic placement of VoIP gateways, your VoIP calls stay on the "free" Internet for as long as possible, jumping onto the PSTN only when necessary to complete the call.

Regulatory Compliance

Public telephone services are heavily regulated by the Federal Communications Commission (FCC) in the United States, and include myriad regulatory issues and orders that must be complied with. For example, mandatory regulations exist for 911 services, rural phone services, accessibility for persons with disabilities, and wiretapping access for police and government agencies (Communications Assistance for Law Enforcement Agencies [CALEA] in the U.S.).

Broadband phone services are not classified by regulators in the same way as standard telephony. Instead, they are classified as data services, and therefore many of the same regulations do not apply (not yet at least—this is currently being challenged by the U.S. traditional telephone companies).

Because VoIP is not currently subject to the same regulations, the recurring operational costs for VoIP providers are less than those of PSTN providers. This is an advantage from a cost perspective, but it might have a downside (see Chapter 4, "Knowing Your Limits.")

Taxes and Fees

Public telephone services are also heavily taxed by the local, state, and federal governments. Really take a close look at your phone bill some day. It contains some of the steepest taxes of anything in our lives, and don't even look at the taxes in your cell phone bill, lest you faint. Taxes and fees tacked onto a typical $59-per-month cell-phone plan include the following:

Federal Universal Service Charge	$1.06
Regulatory Cost Recovery Fee	$0.56
Telecom Relay Service Surcharge	$0.11
Federal Excise Tax	$1.13
State Telecom Sales Tax	$4.04
911 Monthly Fee	$0.70
Total	$7.60

That's roughly 13 percent being tacked onto a cell-phone bill, some of which are charges you probably didn't even know you were paying.

Again, broadband phone services are classified as data services (for today at least), and are therefore not subject to many of the same local, state, and federal taxes. I think we can safely say that this is a temporary condition. We have already seen several studies done by state governments that pointed out how much tax revenue states stand to lose by widespread VoIP service adoption. But for now, enjoy the hole in the tax code.

Phone Number Flexibility

Broadband phone services offer a number of cool options related to phone numbers. For example, with most VoIP providers, you can keep your existing phone number from the traditional phone system if you switch over. In addition a couple of cool options also exist for virtual numbers. The sections that follow discuss these options in greater detail.

Keeping Your Same Phone Number

In Chapter 1, "Traditional Phone Systems," we mention something called Local Number Portability (LNP). Recall that for a long time, a PSTN switch had a set of numbers assigned to it so that if you moved (even if it was a local move, say within the same town), you were probably forced to get a new phone number. Many people were reluctant to go out and pursue a different phone service provider because they didn't want their friends and family to have to learn a new number. This was true for both wired and wireless phone services.

This changed in the United States with the passing of legislation in 1996 (many countries passed similar laws about the same time). Although it took several years to roll out, the advent of LNP means that people can now move across town and keep the same phone number. The following figure shows how number portability works. Suppose the subscriber with phone number 444-555-1002 changes his local phone service to a different provider and chooses to keep his same phone number (with LNP). An entry is created for that subscriber in the Number Portability Administration Center (NPAC) database with the phone number and the real location of the subscriber in the phone network.

Local Number Portability

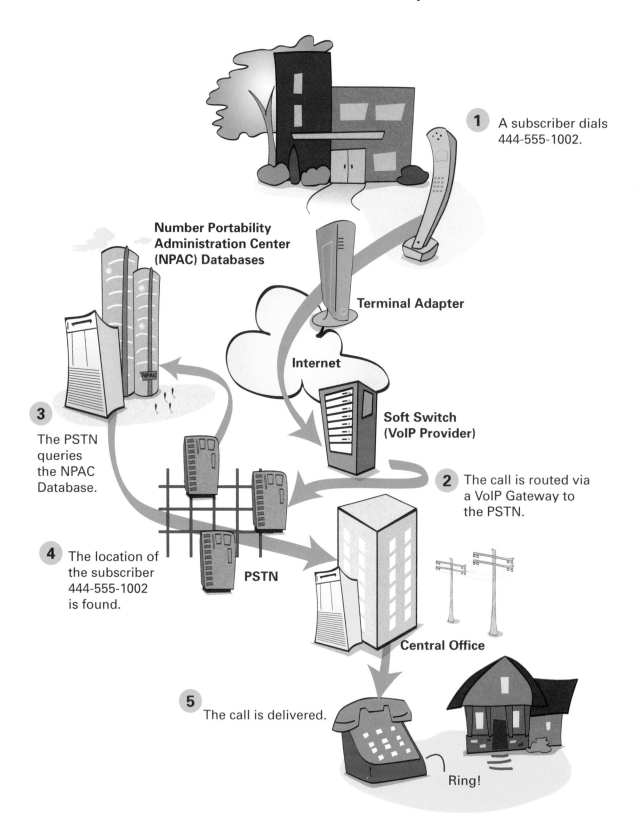

1 A subscriber dials 444-555-1002.

Terminal Adapter

Number Portability Administration Center (NPAC) Databases

Internet

Soft Switch (VoIP Provider)

3 The PSTN queries the NPAC Database.

2 The call is routed via a VoIP Gateway to the PSTN.

4 The location of the subscriber 444-555-1002 is found.

PSTN

Central Office

5 The call is delivered.

Ring!

Now when a caller dials 444-555-1002, the phone system queries the NPAC database to obtain the real location of the called phone, and then routes the call to the appropriate central office for completion. This is very similar to the way 800-number services have worked for many years.

So with any local phone service change, whether wired, wireless, or broadband phone service, you have the option to keep your existing phone number (sometimes for a small one-time fee). This makes switching to a broadband phone service (or any other service) pretty painless for you and your callers. It is worth noting that it physically takes about 1 minute to make the database change, but the request can take up to 30 days to work its way through the system. You might not always be able to keep the same number, so check with your provider to see whether your number can be transferred or whether you must select a new one.

Virtual Phone Numbers

We already discussed that when using broadband phone services, all outgoing calls (local or long-distance) are already included in your monthly rate. However, what about when your friends and family call you? They might still be on the PSTN and be getting a long-distance charge for calls to you. Fortunately (for them) you can get a virtual phone number.

Because you are using the Internet as your phone system, your phone number is no longer tied to a specific geographic location. Your phone (really your terminal adapter) is known by an IP address, much like your computer or home router. Because of this, your actual phone can be close to other phones with similar exchange numbers on the public telephone network, or it can be thousands of miles away. There is really no difference from the broadband phone service provider's point of view. You are simply a device on the Internet with an address.

 We know of several examples of companies and individuals signing up for virtual numbers in the U.S., taking their VoIP terminal adapter back to another country, and still having good voice quality. Their friends and family members in the U.S. can call them internationally for the price of a local call (usually free). VoIP terminal adapters can be plugged in anywhere on the planet where Internet service is available.

Because of this flexibility, the concept of *virtual phone numbers* was created. This allows you to pick a broadband phone number practically anywhere you like—in other towns and even in other area codes. Your single phone line always has a primary phone number, but then you can choose as many additional phone numbers as you need (you are charged a fee for each extra number). You can pick pretty much any number you want as long as someone else is not using it.

The implications of this are pretty big because it not only allows you to make free calls over long distances, but it also allows you to use a phone number that is local to people who call you frequently. This essentially gives them free long-distance service when they call you. For example, suppose that you live in Seattle, Washington, and your grandparents live in West Palm Beach, Florida, as shown in the following figure.

Virtual Phone Numbers

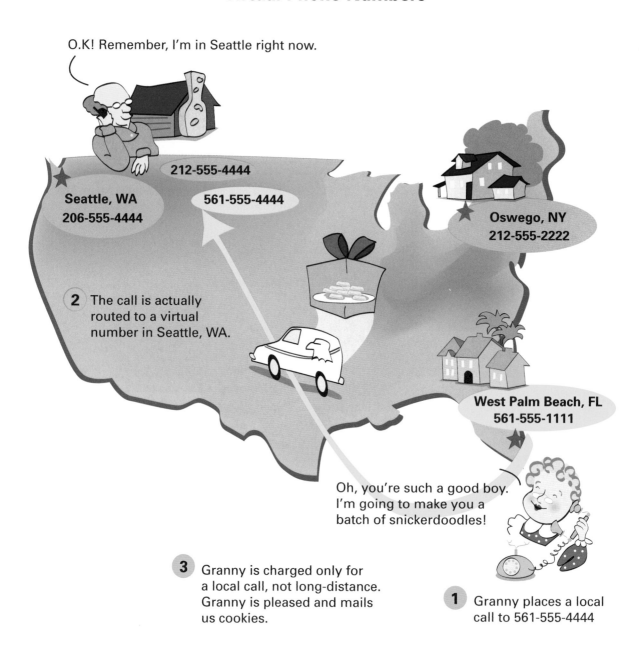

This is about as far apart as two phones can be and still be in the continental United States.. Let's also assume that your granny in Florida likes to call you every day to check up on you. If you both have a VoIP phone, all your calls are free, but if Granny sticks with a PSTN phone (for example, 561-555-1111), the fact that you get free long-distance doesn't help her much. With VoIP, you can request a phone number from the West Palm Beach area (for example, 561-555-4444) so that when Granny calls you, she dials a local number and incurs no charge, no matter how long she talks.

Virtual numbers are pretty neat. One limitation we have found is that outgoing calls from you always have the primary phone number as the calling party. There does not seem to be a way to have any of the virtual numbers appear on someone elses caller ID.

Another issue with virtual numbers is that because of their popularity and a general shortage of phone numbers in some area codes, virtual numbers might not be available in certain area codes. Do your research upfront to see whether you can get the numbers you want. Most of the VoIP providers that offer virtual numbers have a page on their website where you can check the number or area code you want to see whether virtual phone numbers are available.

Online Call Management

A number of pretty neat features are also provided for broadband phone services. These features are not necessarily exclusive to broadband services, but the nature of the service being tied to the Internet does seem to make it easier to deploy and use. The next few sections discuss these features in more detail.

Voice Mail

Voice mail is typically offered by a broadband phone provider as a standard service (although some providers do charge for it). Voice messages are stored in digital form on disk-storage devices at the broadband phone provider, kind of like a sound file is stored on your computer.

Then to check your messages, you have a couple of possibilities. You can listen to the message over the phone by dialing a special code. You could also log on to the provider's web page, click the message in your inbox, and listen to it using your computer. In most cases, you can even send the voice message in an e-mail as an attachment. Finally, you can usually set up an option to send you an e-mail or a page notifying you of a new voice message.

Call Forwarding

Call forwarding is a feature that you have probably become familiar with in the traditional phone system. You will find a few small differences with broadband phone services.

First, you can manage the forwarding online with the click of a button on a web page. Second, you can typically do a bit fancier forwarding, such as regularly scheduled forwarding or advance scheduling. For example, you can set up forwarding to occur during a week-long vacation you have planned.

Finally, one important feature is typically called *offline* or *out-of-service* forwarding. This means that in the event your broadband phone service is either not working or perhaps your home network is not turned on, a number can be set up to receive calls in the event that your broadband phone cannot receive the call.

Call Logs

Very common with broadband phone services is the idea of a call log that you can use to view and manage calls online using a web page. Therefore, you can view incoming calls you received as well as calls that you placed. This service could certainly be provided for traditional phone services (it often is for cell-phone accounts), but it seems to be pretty standard for broadband phone services.

Click to Dial

In addition to viewing incoming and outgoing calls, one interesting feature you can use with a broadband phone service is called *click to dial*. With this feature, you can go online to your call log on the web page, click a number, click **Dial,** and the phone service calls the number. This is just an alternative to manual dialing.

Similarly, with some services, you can establish an address book online that includes phone numbers, and you can click to dial these numbers from the address book as well as the call log.

 One question we often get asked is whether someone can listen in on our phone calls if she hacks her way into an online VoIP account. The short answer is no, you cannot listen to calls in progress from an online account-management website. However, someone might be able to listen to a voice mail stored there, so protect your account and password information just like you would any other valuable online asset.

Summary of Advantages

We have discussed several advantages of broadband phone services over traditional PSTN phone services, including lower cost, flexible phone numbers, and advanced features leveraging the Internet.

Chapter 4 discusses a few limitations. You will then have detailed information to make a decision about whether broadband phone services are right for you, and if so, how you should take advantage of them.

Knowing Your Limits

Along with all sunshine, a little rain must fall. You need to be aware of some limitations of broadband phone services. Two major categories of limitations exist: reliability and 911 services. These are discussed in the sections that follow.

Reliability

As we discussed in Chapter 1, "Traditional Phone Systems," the public switched telephone network (PSTN) has been designed, engineered, and reengineered to achieve the five 9s of reliability (also known as 99.999 percent uptime). In real terms, this means that, on average, the system has no more than about 5 minutes of downtime per year. For the most part, the PSTN lives up to this incredible standard.

So the obvious question is "Are broadband phone services as reliable as the PSTN?" The short answer is this: No they are not, but keep in mind that the five 9s is a really high standard. But perhaps a better question to ask is this: "Are broadband phone services reliable enough for you?" We can break down the service into the following three major components that can affect reliability:

- The terminal adapter, including electric power
- Broadband Internet service and the broader Internet
- Broadband phone service provider infrastructure, switches, and gateways

Hypothetically speaking, assume that the broadband phone service infrastructure (meaning Voice over IP (VoIP) soft switches, gateways, and so on) is nearly as reliable as the public telephone system infrastructure, or it will be in the near future. This leaves the broadband Internet service and the terminal adapter to consider.

It's Electric

As we discuss in Chapter 2, "Voice over IP (VoIP)," one of the most important differences with broadband phone services is that while the public telephone system's central office provides power to the handsets in your home, broadband phone services are powered by the terminal adapter, which is plugged into the power outlet in your home. So if your home is without power, so is your terminal adapter, and your broadband phone service is not going to function.

Similarly, your broadband Internet modem (whether DSL or cable) also gets its power from your home, so if the power is out, your Internet service is going to be out as well. Central office systems in the PSTN often have a power backup generator to keep the system functioning for some period during a widespread power outage. Broadband services typically do not.

An uninterruptible power supply (UPS) can keep your cable modem and terminal adapter running for a short period of time, but we are talking hours, not days. If you live in an area with frequent power outages, a generator can be a good solution for keeping your VoIP service up and running.

This is obviously a pretty significant limitation that needs to be considered if you are thinking about replacing your PSTN line with a broadband phone service. It might not be too big a deal to lose a secondary phone line. It could be a very big deal to lose your only line.

Reliance on Broadband and the Internet

When the Internet was first getting started, the speed and reliability of the system were both insufficient for voice communication. In recent years, however, the switches and routers that move data across the Internet have been upgraded to the point that even with the dramatic increase of data traffic, the Internet can handle it just fine. The general reliability of the Internet has also been greatly improved, mostly because so many businesses now rely on the Internet.

With these improvements, the slowest and least reliable part of the Internet is now the section between your provider and your home. This section of the network is commonly referred to as the *last mile*. This makes sense if you think about it in terms of a water system. The big pipes in the core of the system closest to the water supply are well maintained, probably with redundant pipes for backups. But as you get farther out to the individual pipes on each street, you have less reliability.

Also, you have the problem of *aggregation,* which means bringing thousands of smaller pipes into one big pipe. Imagine if a water system had to be designed in your town so that every household could simultaneously run its water wide open in every faucet. Obviously that would be cost prohibitive, so the system is designed using assumptions of how many people will use the water at the same time. The Internet and broadband systems are similar. They are designed assuming that not everyone will use their connection to its maximum, simultaneously. (By the way, the PSTN is designed with similar assumptions.)

All things being equal, the available broadband Internet services definitely vary, with some being much better than others. In general, they are all improving, and if you have a bad experience with one (say, DSL) try another (say, cable). The bottom line is, we have found the majority of today's broadband companies to be very capable of supporting broadband phone services with high quality.

 It is worth mentioning that satellite services are marketed as "broadband" Internet access, but they are not really suitable for VoIP. The uplink bandwidth is usually relatively low, and the end-to-end delay of going up and down to and from a satellite can be significant.

Note Sometimes the reliability of the PSTN is a bit of a false comfort. One of our favorite tales is a true story that happened after a large ice storm in North Carolina. A fellow we work with had to call his PSTN provider on his broadband phone line to report his PSTN phone outage.

The point is this: Outages can affect any service. Probably the best approach is to have multiple types of phone services (such as VoIP, cell, and/or PSTN); that way, if you lose one, you can try the other.

Voice Quality

The quality of a voice conversation on the PSTN is mainly determined by the distance over which you are calling, the quality of the wiring between the two points, the quality of the network serving you, the called party, and all things in between.

The quality of a voice conversation over a broadband phone service can be affected by some of the same things. In addition, the nature of the voice conversation being carried over a packet-switched network (see Chapter 2) offers a few new challenges. The quality of a VoIP conversation comes down to the following four things:

- **Bandwidth**—Is my broadband connection fast enough to handle all the VoIP packets I need to send and receive?

- **Delay**—Will my VoIP packets get there fast enough?

- **Loss**—How many VoIP packets will arrive too slowly, or not at all?

- **Equipment quality**—If you buy a cheap handset, it can impact your quality. This does not mean that you need to buy a $400 phone, but if you pull a $5 phone out of a box at a garage sale, don't expect to hear CD-quality audio.

A picture might help you to understand. As shown in the following figure, you need to have enough *bandwidth* on your broadband Internet service to carry a VoIP conversation plus all the other data (such as e-mail, web browsing, and so on) that you want to send and receive. In general, a single VoIP conversation uses approximately 90 kbps. A typical broadband speed that you can get from your provider is 384 kbps (uplink). This means you have 90 kbps for VoIP and 294 kbps for data. That should work out pretty well.

If you or people in your house use applications on the web that consume a lot of bandwidth in the uplink direction (from your house to the Internet), such as hosting file sharing or sending lots of very large e-mail attachments, it could affect your voice quality.

Typically most high-bandwidth applications, such as streaming video, music downloads, and so on, are in the downlink direction (from the Internet to your house) and do not affect voice quality very often. This is because your broadband Internet downlink speed is typically much higher than the uplink, often 1.5 Mbps, 2 Mbps, or higher.

By the way, some VoIP services, such as Time Warner Cable's Digital Voice line, have dedicated bandwidth for the VoIP call between your house and the Internet, so they are not affected by the computer applications on your home network.

Voice Quality on a VoIP Call

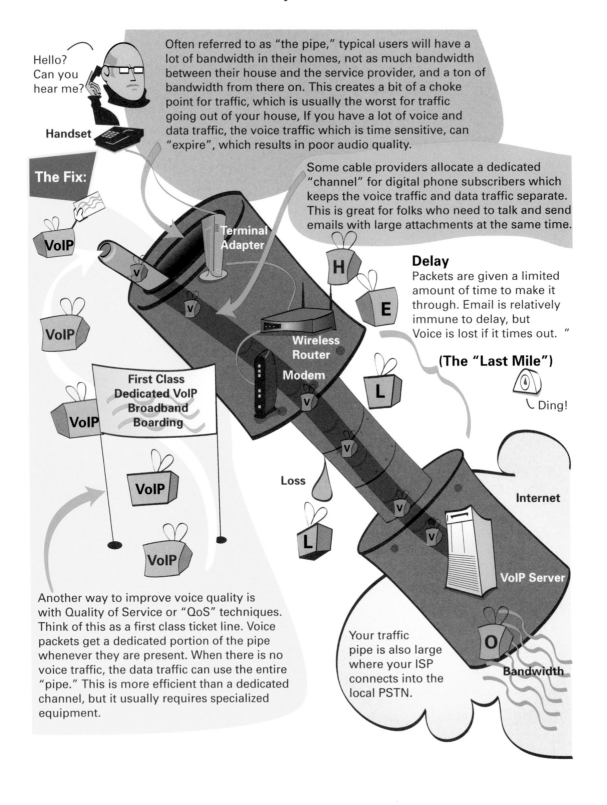

Hello? Can you hear me?

Handset

Often referred to as "the pipe," typical users will have a lot of bandwidth in their homes, not as much bandwidth between their house and the service provider, and a ton of bandwidth from there on. This creates a bit of a choke point for traffic, which is usually the worst for traffic going out of your house, If you have a lot of voice and data traffic, the voice traffic which is time sensitive, can "expire", which results in poor audio quality.

Some cable providers allocate a dedicated "channel" for digital phone subscribers which keeps the voice traffic and data traffic separate. This is great for folks who need to talk and send emails with large attachments at the same time.

The Fix:

VoIP

VoIP

Terminal Adapter

Delay
Packets are given a limited amount of time to make it through. Email is relatively immune to delay, but Voice is lost if it times out. "

Wireless Router Modem

(The "Last Mile")

Ding!

First Class Dedicated VoIP Broadband Boarding

VoIP

VoIP

Loss

Internet

VoIP

VoIP Server

Another way to improve voice quality is with Quality of Service or "QoS" techniques. Think of this as a first class ticket line. Voice packets get a dedicated portion of the pipe whenever they are present. When there is no voice traffic, the data traffic can use the entire "pipe." This is more efficient than a dedicated channel, but it usually requires specialized equipment.

Your traffic pipe is also large where your ISP connects into the local PSTN.

Bandwidth

Delay refers to the length of time it takes packets to travel from your terminal adapter, across the Internet, to the other terminal adapter (or possible gateway to the PSTN). If your broadband provider's network is not fast enough, you could experience delay that would degrade voice quality. After you are on the Internet, speed is likely not to be an issue (the Internet backbone has almost no delay). Most broadband providers we have experience with are plenty fast. A small number of providers have serious issues in their networks that need to be addressed, and if you are unlucky enough to be using one of them, you might have a problem. You can find feedback from other consumers on different providers at http://www.broadbandreports.com.

Finally, *loss* of the VoIP packets can cause voice quality issues also. Under normal circumstances, you only lose a very small number of packets (for example, 1 in 10,000), which is not noticeable during a VoIP call. Loss of several packets in succession might be noticeable, causing you to hear "choppy" speech, "garbled" speech, or missing syllables or words. Typically, packet-loss problems occur only when a widespread outage exists in the broadband network itself, or some similar service-affecting outage.

In summary, voice quality on a broadband phone service can be better than that on the PSTN. It could also be closer to cell-phone quality. VoIP providers are getting better every day. In our opinion, each family needs to evaluate how and what they will use the service for and how critical the quality of the service is for their situation. We use it and have had very good voice quality approximately 98 percent of the time.

 Here's an odd fact: With the traditional public telephone system, most people considered the slight background noise to be an indication of a good connection (despite the fact that it is really an indication of compromised sound quality). Because most of the world's phone users trained theselves over the years to hear this noise, the absence of such noise on a digital phone connection really bothers people and makes most wonder whether the connection is still live (Hello?). To mitigate this "problem," digital systems inject static on the receiving end (making the sound a lower quality than it actually is) to let users know that they still have a good connection. This injected static is referred to as *comfort noise.*

911 and E911

So the free stuff is one thing, but safety is critical, particularly if you are thinking about swapping your PSTN phone out and going exclusively with a VoIP phone. This section discusses everything you need to know about 911 services (or the equivalent emergency number services in your country) and VoIP.

How 911 and E911 Works

Let's start with a basic understanding of how 911 services work. When you dial 9-1-1, your call is immediately routed to a Public Safety Answering Point (PSAP). The PSAP is staffed by trained emergency dispatchers, who can route the appropriate public safety officers (fire, police, and rescue) to you depending on the nature of your emergency, as illustrated in the following figure. When 911 systems first came online, the system depended on verbal communication with the dispatchers, and then, as today, many emergency dispatchers had a hand in saving lives.

How 911 and E911 Systems Work

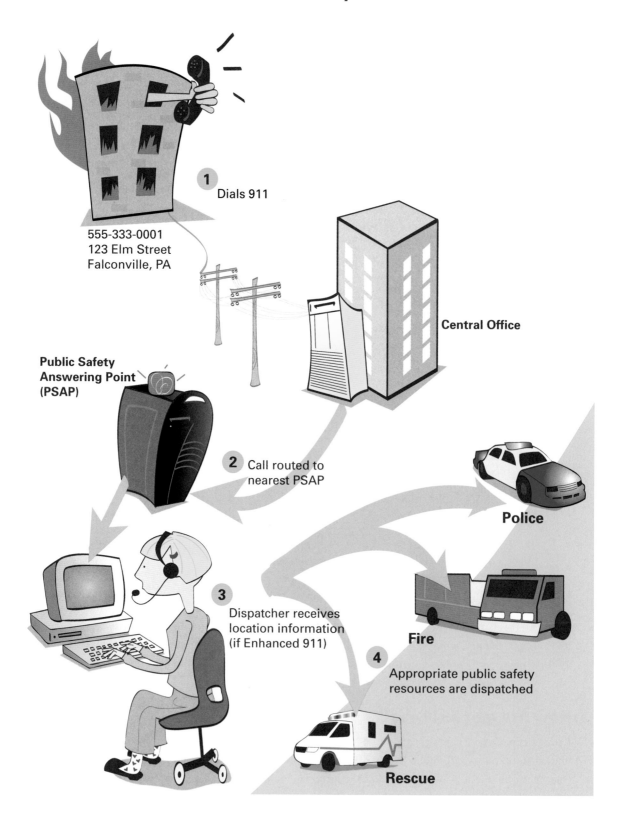

1 Dials 911

555-333-0001
123 Elm Street
Falconville, PA

Central Office

**Public Safety
Answering Point
(PSAP)**

2 Call routed to
nearest PSAP

Police

3 Dispatcher receives
location information
(if Enhanced 911)

Fire

4 Appropriate public safety
resources are dispatched

Rescue

In modern 911 systems, the dispatch is also provided with information regarding the caller on their computer screen. This information includes the name of the account holder (remember that the account holder is not always the person that calls), the address, the phone number, and in some cases, specialized instructions. This means that if someone calls 911, the dispatcher is immediately provided with the phone number and the physical location of the caller (keeping in mind, we are referring to the PSTN, not cellular/wireless or VoIP service).

Even if the caller becomes incapacitated after dialing, if he cannot speak, or if he is unable to communicate who and where he is for some other reason (for example, if a small child dials after one of his parents gets hurt), the dispatcher can still do her job. If your system has this capability (it's called Enhanced 911 [E911], and most communities in the United States have it), you just need to dial 9-1-1, and help will come to you even if you never speak a word.

It's a fantastic system, and in a world of frustration with our local, state, and federal governments, we sometimes overlook the unbelievably hard work and ingenuity that has gone into our public systems such as the E911 system.

The Challenge for VoIP

One of the first issues with 911 service over VoIP is related to the portability that we discuss in Chapter 3, "Advantages of Broadband Phone Services." Recall the example in Chapter 3 where we opted for a West Palm Beach, Florida virtual number even though we were living in Seattle. If you dialed 9-1-1 from that VoIP phone in Seattle, who do you suppose would answer the call—the dispatcher in West Palm Beach or the one in Seattle?

This is a critical problem, because even if you were able to tell the emergency dispatcher who and where you were, and the nature of the emergency, if you are not talking to someone in your local PSAP, the dispatcher might not be able to contact the public safety folks in your local area. In fact, the farther the PSAP you talk to is away from your local PSAP, the harder it will probably be for the dispatcher to help, because PSAPs are not on a common network. So, if you are in Seattle and you reach the West Palm Beach PSAP, unless the nature of your problem can be solved over the phone, you are in trouble.

Another issue is that VoIP phones (along with their associated phone numbers) are physically portable, so you can literally pick up your handset and terminal adapter and connect them to any place with Internet access, in another house, town, and so on, and the number follows you. So even if the local PSAP knew who and where you were before the move, if you move the phone, the ambulance is going to show up where you were, rather than where you are. You can also take a PSTN handset anywhere, but the phone number is tied to the house, not the phone, so on the PSTN, a 911 dispatcher can still find you.

By the way, this is similar to the problem that the cellular/wireless phone service providers are dealing with today. They are working hard to be able to automatically identify where a mobile user is calling 911 from, so that a form of E911 service can be provided, even when a mobile phone is... well...mobile.

Solutions

First and foremost, you should understand that broadband phone service providers are working as part of a national task force to bring E911 services to VoIP systems. By the time you read this, it might not even be an issue for you. Many broadband phone services already provide you with an option to register your broadband phone number with your local PSAP. This is great news, particularly if you choose a VoIP phone number from a city that's far away from your current residence. With this registration, no matter what number you have, you can still reach the PSAP for your local area.

However, not all VoIP systems are tied into the PSAP systems. When you dial 9-1-1 from a VoIP phone, your call might be routed as illustrated in the following figure.

In this case, a broadband phone subscriber dials 9-1-1. The call is routed to a special 911 service provided by the broadband phone service company, where an agent speaks to you and looks up your location information. Then this agent typically places a call to your local PSAP administrative line rather than the main system line. The administrative line is manned by an emergency dispatcher, but this line does not provide the dispatcher with your name, number, and location. This of course means that if you can't talk, the dispatcher would have a difficult time assessing where you are or what the nature of your emergency is. Now we don't want to make this sound all bad, because being connected to the right PSAP is a huge improvement over the alternative, but while good, it's still not the same as calling from a PSTN line.

Caution Don't forget to read the "It's Electric" section, earlier in this chapter. Your broadband phone service is most likely not going to work when you have no electricity at your home. This means that you will also likely not be able to dial 9-1-1 from the broadband phone handset during a power outage.

In the United States (as well as other countries), legislation was passed requiring VoIP providers to give their subscribers detailed information on their 911 services, capabilities, and limitations. When you sign up for service, the broadband phone provider can give you information on which type of 911 (or E911) solution it provides.

In most countries where VoIP is widespread and growing, a time line has been imposed for VoIP providers to tie into the E911 system so that the PSAP dispatchers can see your information whether you are calling from a PSTN phone or a VoIP phone.

Caution Even when your VoIP system is integrated into the public safety system and E911 services are offered, the problem with moving your broadband phone handset and terminal adapter remains. So it is important not to relocate your broadband phone equipment without notifying your provider of the new location.

How Some VoIP Systems Handle 911 Calls

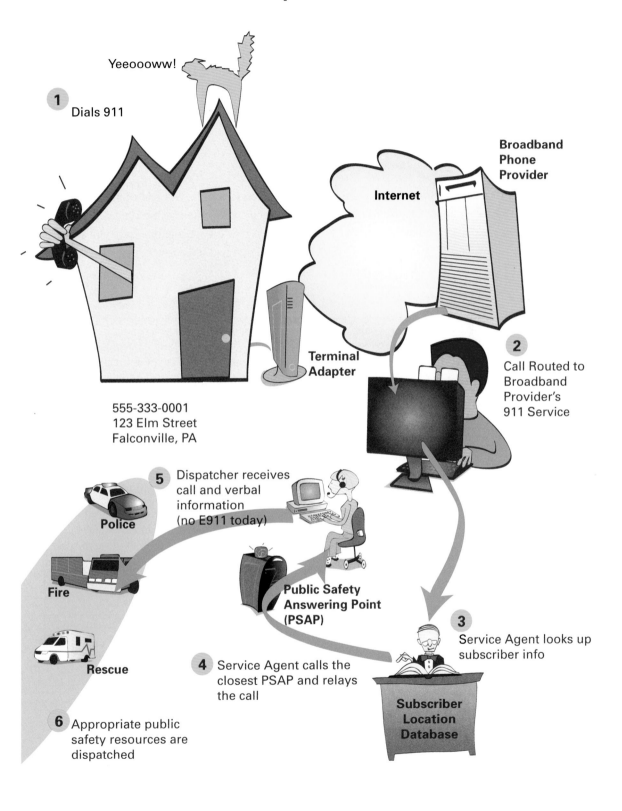

1 Dials 911

Yeeooooww!

Broadband Phone Provider

Internet

Terminal Adapter

555-333-0001
123 Elm Street
Falconville, PA

2 Call Routed to Broadband Provider's 911 Service

5 Dispatcher receives call and verbal information (no E911 today)

Police

Fire

Public Safety Answering Point (PSAP)

Rescue

3 Service Agent looks up subscriber info

4 Service Agent calls the closest PSAP and relays the call

Subscriber Location Database

6 Appropriate public safety resources are dispatched

One final word on 911: Regardless of the level of reliance you plan on having on VoIP, from a single phone in a home office to a complete switchover, the smart thing to do is to educate yourself and your family on the limitations of emergency services over VoIP phones. This should include informing houseguests, babysitters, caregivers, and employees should you have them in your home. The worst time to discover the limitations of a system is in the heat of an emergency.

Ask your (intended) VoIP provider what services it provides for emergency calling. It's now federal law (in the United States) for the VoIP provider to have you acknowledge that it has informed you of its emergency call–handling services when you sign up.

Table 4-1 summarizes the current status of 911 and E911 services for different types of phone services (landline PSTN, cellular/mobile, and VoIP) at the time this book was written (in the United States). By Federal Communications Commission (FCC) mandate, all systems are moving relatively quickly toward full support of E911 services, but they are in different stages of implementation.

Table 4-1   Comparison of Emergency Calling Services (in the U.S.)

	Basic 911—Dialing 9-1-1 connects caller to nearest PSAP	**Enhanced 911 (E911)—Dialing 9-1-1 connects caller to nearest PSAP, provides calling party number and other information to automatically determine callers location and callback number**
Landline (PSTN)	Widely available	Widely available
Wireless (cellular/mobile)	Widely available	Rolling out in two phases: Phase I (nearly complete)—Calling party number and automatic location to the cell tower used to place the call Phase II (future)—Refine automatic location to within 50–300 yards of the caller
VoIP	Widely available; check with your VoIP provider for limitations	Still in development; check with your VoIP provider

Summary of Limitations

Broadband phone services have many advantages over PSTN services, but also have significant limitations. If you understand the limitations, you can make an informed decision about how to use these services to your best advantage.

VoIP calls can range in quality from cell-phone quality to PSTN equivalent. Your VoIP phone generally only works when your home has power. In VoIP service, 911 and E911 services are still evolving to be equivalent to those of the PSTN service. These emergency services can be fantastic if they are used appropriately.

It is important to note our assumptions in the chart. In this case, we are assuming that high-speed Internet access is $50 per month and that our monthly long-distance bill is $25 per month on average. The chart does not include the "value" of high-speed Internet beyond its monthly cost. Keep these things in mind when looking at the chart and plug in your own costs if they are different than the ones shown.

 # From the Geek Squad Files

Okay, so you've heard all the hype about Internet telephony and you are ready to take the plunge. As with all the high-tech stuff we see, install, tame, and repair, the number-one thing users can do to save themselves some grief is to understand what they are getting into. (This book is a great first step!)

Internet telephony is great and the free long-distance is fabulous. If we had girlfriends who lived out of state (or anywhere, really) we would call them all the time using Voice over IP (VoIP). However, some limitations do exist. Here are some reminders (this might seem redundant, but we hear about this stuff all the time):

- **Power**—If you lose power, you will lose your Internet telephony service, unless you have back-up power (you might still lose your Internet service). So as a reminder, if you lose power, you will not be able to use your Internet phone. In other words, no power = no phone (we really do hear about this one a lot). In addition to this, you could have power, but if your cable is out, your phone is probably not working either. Check the lights on your modem to be sure. One final note: Be sure that your other appliances are working before assuming that your VoIP service is out.

- **Quality**—In general, the quality of your Internet phone will not be the same as that of a land-line. You might experience a "glitch" once in a while, but when your VoIP service is working, it sounds just fine.

- **Emergency services**—Emergency services range from nothing to full Enhanced 911 (E911) services. Just understand what you are getting into. The VoIP providers are required to have you read and agree that you understanding their capabilities. Instead of simply scrolling down to the bottom of the screen and clicking the **Accept** button, we suggest that you actually read any disclaimers.

- **Cost**—This technology might not save you as much money as you think. If you never or rarely use long-distance, you might not save much. Do some quick calculations and make sure that VoIP is right for you and that you are not just following the herd. You should probably figure out your average bill over a year, rather than just look at your largest single bill.

- **Power**—If you lose power, you will lose your Internet phone service. Really.

PART **II**

PART II

Choosing an Internet Phone Service

With Part I behind us, you should now have a good grasp on what VoIP is, how it works, and how it's different from the PSTN. Now we take a deeper look at what the various VoIP services are, how to determine whether this technology is right for you, how to chose the right service provider, and what equipment you will need if you decide that VoIP is the right choice for you.

The first thing to do now is to learn about the different types of VoIP. Chapter 6, "Inventory of Broadband Phone Services," provides an list of VoIP services and gives you a summary of the advantages and limitations of each type. We also provide some pointers to most of the major providers so that you can see which services are available in your area and what the current packages and prices are.

Armed with an understanding of what is available, you need to determine which VoIP service, if any, is right for you. In Chapter 7, "Selecting an Internet Phone Service," we walk you through this decision so that you can determine whether you will save money by switching and whether certain limitations or advantages of the various VoIP services would sway your opinion.

If you are still reading the book at Chapter 8, "Selecting VoIP Equipment," you have probably decided to go ahead with a VoIP service or you are one of our moms (Hi Mom!). Chapter 8 is all about how determining what equipment you need. In some cases, the service provider can give you everything you need (except the phone), but this is not always the case. Much of this depends on where and how you plan to use VoIP.

CHAPTER 6

Inventory of Broadband Phone Services

This chapter briefly takes a look at different types of broadband phone services. After you have a basic understanding of how to sort out the different service types, we move on to Chapter 7, "Selecting an Internet Phone Service," which discusses how to select a service.

The following three primary types of broadband phone services exist:

- Internet VoIP phone services
- Cable VoIP digital phone services
- VoIP chat services

The similarities and differences among these types of service are discussed in the sections that follow.

Internet VoIP Phone Services

Internet VoIP phone services include any service that can provide phone services over the Internet. These services are popular for providing low-cost additional phone lines to homes. Typically, the service has components like those shown in Figure 6-1.

Figure 6-1   Internet VoIP Phone Services

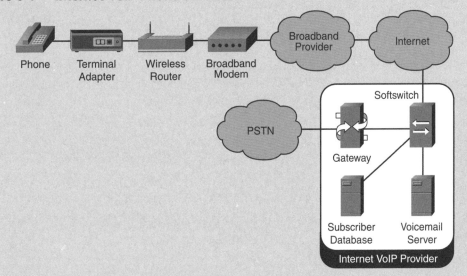

In the home, you would have a terminal adapter (also referred to as an Analog Terminal Adapter, or ATA), which would enable the phone handsets in your home to work with digital VoIP. High-speed broadband Internet access provides the connection to your phone provider.

At the provider, a *softswitch* (a big computer) typically acts as the central office to route calls to and from phones. There is usually a subscriber database and a voice-mail server, as well as a gateway to the public switched telephone network (PSTN) for "off-Net" calls (that is, calls that originate or terminate on a different network than the broadband phone service provider's).

With this type of service, you are assigned a phone number, and your dialing is nearly identical to that of the PSTN. Features provided are also similar to the PSTN, with the additional features described in Chapter 3, "Advantages of Broadband Phone Services." Costs range from $10 to $50 per month, depending on the features included and whether unlimited local and long-distance calls are included.

Table 6-1 presents some examples of this type of phone service. (Note that it would take a separate book to list all of them, but this table lists some of the most popular.)

Table 6-1   Common Residential Internet VoIP Service Providers

Internet VoIP Service Provider	Store Signup	Online Signup	Website
AT&T CallVantage	Yes	Yes	http://www.callvantage.com
EarthLink trueVoice	No	Yes	http://www.earthlink.net/voice
Lingo	No	Yes	http://www.lingo.com
Packet8	No	Yes	http://www.packet8.com
SunRocket	No	Yes	http://www.sunrocket.com
Verizon Voicewing	No	Yes	http://www.voicewing.com
Vonage	Yes	Yes	http://www.vonage.com

Cable VoIP Digital Phone Services

Cable VoIP phone services are similar to Internet VoIP services (actually they are kind of a subset). The primary difference is that your cable provider, which typically provides you with high-speed broadband Internet access, also provides you with a VoIP-based digital phone service. These services are increasingly popular as a replacement for your primary PSTN line. Typically the service has components like those shown in Figure 6-2.

Figure 6-2   Cable VoIP Phone Services

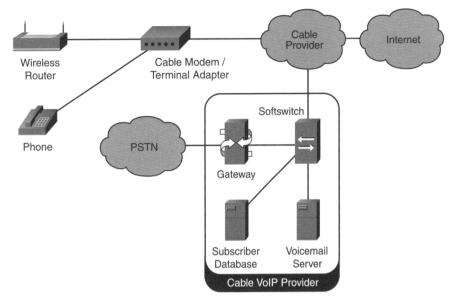

In this case, the broadband cable modem usually serves a dual role, also acting as the terminal adapter that converts the handsets in your home to digital VoIP. High-speed broadband Internet access provides the connection to your phone provider.

Just as with an Internet VoIP provider, a softswitch would typically act as the central office to route calls to and from phones. There is usually a subscriber database and a voice-mail server, as well as a gateway to the PSTN for "off-Net" calls (that is, calls that originate or terminate on a different network than the cable VoIP service provider's).

With this type of service, you are also assigned a phone number, and your dialing is nearly identical to that of the PSTN. Features provided are also similar to the PSTN, with the additional features described in Chapter 3.

What differentiates a cable VoIP service is that your high-speed broadband cable provider is also the VoIP provider. In this case, calls are not typically transported across the public Internet, but instead are routed directly from the broadband cable network to the VoIP switch. Costs range from $40 to $60, depending on the features included and whether unlimited local and long-distance calls are included.

 It's worth mentioning that even if you get Internet access from a cable provider that offers VoIP service, you can choose VoIP from a different provider.

Most cable providers offer a form of cable VoIP service, including those shown in Table 6-2. Cable providers are specific to your geographic area; this table lists some of the largest in the United States.

Table 6-2   Common Residential Cable VoIP Service Providers

Cable VoIP Service Provider	Website
Cablevision Optimum Voice	http://www.optimumvoice.com/
Charter Telephone	http://www.charter.com/products/telephone/telephone.aspx
Comcast Home Phone Service	http://www.comcast.com/Products/Telephony/
Cox Digital Telephone	http://www.cox.com/Telephone/
Time Warner Cable Digital Phone	http://www.timewarnercable.com/corporate/products/digitalphone/

VoIP Chat Services

VoIP chat services are a bit different from Internet VoIP and cable VoIP services. While those services operate similarly to PSTN telephone services, including being assigned a normal phone number, VoIP chat services work much more like instant messaging (IM) programs, and are often referred to as *PC-to-PC calling*. These services are rapidly growing as a low-cost method for international calling and are popular with teenagers for general unlimited talking to each other. Typically, the service has components like those shown in Figure 6-3.

Figure 6-3   VoIP Chat Services

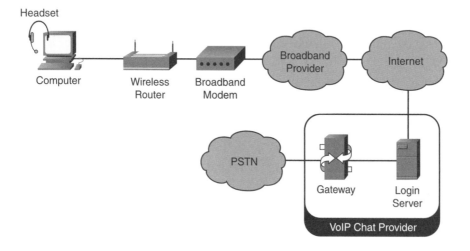

In this case, you have no distinct terminal adapters in your home. The terminal adapter function is provided by a desktop or laptop computer. Another difference is that your computer (or game system, if you use Xbox Live) also usually serves as the handset, and it's generally not a service to which you would connect your traditional PSTN handsets. High-speed broadband Internet access provides the connection to your VoIP chat provider.

Note A wireless handset is available from Linksys (CIT200 Cordless Internet Telephony Kit) that works with one of your home computers as the base. This allows you to access a VoIP chat service (such as Skype) using a cordless phone, instead of using a headset connected to the computer.

With this type of service, you are usually *not* assigned a phone number. Your typically method of calling each other is to look up the person in the contact list on your computer and click his or her name, similar to IM. With some services, you can call PSTN phone numbers as well (usually at a premium charge). The features provided are typically similar to IM features, not the fancier PSTN features found in Internet VoIP or cable VoIP services. Calls are typically free to other users on the service, and you are charged for "off-Net" calls, for example, to the PSTN. Chapter 15, "VoIP Chat Services," covers VoIP chat services in greater detail.

There are a growing number of providers that offer VoIP chat services. Table 6-3 lists the most common ones.

Table 6-3   Common VoIP Chat Service Providers

VoIP Chat Service Provider	Website
AOL Instant Messenger	http://www.aim.com/
Google Talk	http://www.google.com/talk/
MSN Messenger	http://messenger.msn.com
Skype	http://www.skype.com
Yahoo! Messenger	http://messenger.yahoo.com/

Summary of Broadband Phone Services

Several types of broadband phone services are available, each with different capabilities. They fall into two broad categories: those that work like the PSTN and even work with your PSTN handsets (Internet VoIP and cable VoIP services), and those that work more like IM and use your home computer as the handset.

Confused yet? It's true that you have a lot of VoIP options to choose from. Table 6-4 provides a quick summary of these options.

Table 6-4   Quick Comparison of VoIP Service Types

Type	Advantages	Limitations
Internet VoIP	Works similarly to a PSTN line and uses existing handsets Choose from a number of providers Relatively low cost Can be added as an alternative line to a primary PSTN line Can often keep existing phone number	Voice quality can sometimes be affected by other traffic on your home network
Cable VoIP	Works similarly to a PSTN line and uses existing handsets Voice quality can be very high; the VoIP bandwidth is usually dedicated on your broadband connection Can often keep existing phone number	Limited choice of providers, because your local cable TV company is typically the only option
VoIP chat	Choose from a number of providers Cost is free or cheap Available anywhere you take your laptop	Requires a computer to place phone calls Voice quality varies from good to poor Only reachable when computer is on and logged in to the service No support for 911 or Enhanced 911 (E911) services Must select a new phone number; no porting of existing numbers

By the way, all types of VoIP services have the advantages discussed in Chapter 3 and the limitations discussed in Chapter 4, "Knowing Your Limits." For example, all three have the advantage of being lower cost, and all three have the limitations related to losing power in your house. Table 6-4 simply points out some specific advantages and limitations when comparing the types of VoIP services.

The next chapter dives a bit deeper into how to choose which of these services is right for you, and how to select a service.

CHAPTER 7

Selecting an Internet Phone Service

You have a lot to consider when deciding which broadband phone service(s) are right for you. Trade-offs among cost, reliability, feature richness, and safety make this an important decision. Trying to wade through the marketing on one side and the concerns on the other can also make the decision difficult. This chapter walks you through some of the important things to keep in mind. It should hopefully provide some guidance to help you with the decision.

What Will I Use It For?

A big part of your decision about the Internet phone service(s) you pick depends on exactly how you plan to use it. Possible uses include some or all of the following:

- International calling to friends and family overseas

- National long-distance calling to friends and family

- Second line for your household, for example, for teenagers

- Local calling option for friends and family

- Primary phone line

A common reason that people are seeking out Internet phone services is to lower their long-distance costs. For national long-distance, today you have little reason to be charged for calls. Even many public switched telephone network (PSTN) providers are offering flat-rate telephone services, including unlimited long-distance (national).

Another common scenario, especially for VoIP chat service, is for international calling. Because of the international gateway costs and regulatory differences from country to country, it is still common to be charged for most VoIP services internationally. One exception is VoIP chat service, which when used totally "on-Net" (that is, one computer on the Internet communicating to another), is typically still free. However, you can't expect the same sound quality as you have with a landline call, however, if your friends and family also want to save money, and you can live with the occasional voice quality issue, VoIP chat can be a cost-effective service.

Many people need a second (and even a third) phone line in the house. For homes with teenagers, having a single phone line can be a constant source of frustration for both parents and teenagers. A second PSTN line is possible in most homes (the wiring is often already in place), but it's usually a fairly pricey option. A broadband phone service can be a cost-effective way to add more lines.

Sometimes the long-distance problem is not on our end. Perhaps we already have a flat-rate service, but our friends or family in another city do not, and they pay long-distance charges every time they call us. Saying "too bad, not my problem" is one solution. But the more thoughtful among us might consider a broadband VoIP service with a local number in our friends' city so that they can phone us for unlimited minutes and pay nothing above the cost of their local phone service. Of course, if it's your mother-in-law in that other city, you might want to really think this through first.

Finally, some folks are fed up with their current local PSTN provider and would like to cut the lines in favor of a more permanent alternative for their primary phone service. A cable VoIP service (if it's offered in your area) can be a reasonable alternative. However, please read Chapter 4, "Knowing Your Limits," before you take this step to make sure that you understand the implications of getting a VoIP line. It's not for everyone, although a lot of people are getting one.

 While some online gaming services, such as Xbox Live, have VoIP capability, it is not a general-purpose VoIP service. So while it is great for talking with folks you are playing with or against, you can't use it to dial someone's phone.

What Is My Backup Plan?

When choosing an Internet phone service, we suggest that you think about your telephone communications as a total picture. What are all the possible communication paths you have today, including PSTN, cell phones, and any VoIP services you might already have?

Just having multiple types of services can be a good thing so that if one type of service is out of order, you can simply switch to another. So what is your backup plan in case something goes awry?

Power

Today, if you have only PSTN phones, power might not be an issue. The central office that supplies your phone service will probably continue to have power during relatively short power outages, so you will still have phone service. For extended wide-area power outages, even the PSTN can be compromised, when its backup generators are exhausted or fail.

Many people commonly replace their PSTN handsets with cordless phones. Cordless phones don't work either when the power is out, because they generally require AC power.

For Internet phone services, as we discuss in Chapter 4, power is supplied to the broadband Internet modem, the VoIP terminal adapter, and the phone handset in your home. So if the power goes out in your home, the Internet service is down and so is your VoIP line. A possible solution to this is to make sure that your VoIP equipment can fall back on power from a backup generator (assuming that you already use one for your other electricity needs in the event of an outage). Another possible solution is to purchase a small uninterruptible power supply (UPS).

You plug a UPS into your home power outlet. Then instead of plugging your computer and other equipment into a wall outlet, you plug them into the UPS. When your home has power, the computer receives power through the UPS from the wall outlet. When a power failure occurs, batteries inside the UPS kick in to continue to supply the equipment with power, even though your wall outlet no longer has power. When the batteries are exhausted, the backup power is lost.

For about $200, you can have a small UPS that keeps your equipment functioning for an hour or two after a power failure. If you had cable VoIP service, you would need to plug the cable modem (with integrated VoIP terminal adapter) into the UPS. Then, assuming that a PSTN (cordless base) handset is plugged into it, the UPS could keep the cable VoIP service active. If, however, you had Internet VoIP service, you would need to plug your broadband cable/DSL modem, home network router, and terminal adapter all into the UPS.

Backup Line

Many people seem to forget that they have an excellent backup line already, called a cell phone. We used to worry a lot more about losing our PSTN line. Today, most people call us on our cell phones anyway, even when we are at home.

Remember, the mobile phone system has some of the same challenges with 911 services that VoIP services do (see Chapter 4). If you dial 9-1-1 from your cell phone and can't speak, it might take the dispatcher a few minutes to locate you. Mobile providers are busily deploying solutions in their networks so that they can automatically locate a cell phone in their network to within a hundred feet or so (thanks to a Federal Communications Commission [FCC] mandate).

Still, if your PSTN or VoIP line is out of order, a cell phone can be a great backup line.

Keeping a Minimal PSTN Line

Some people consider VoIP services and, because of the potential issues we mention in the preceding paragraphs, opt to keep a minimal PSTN line. This can be a good approach. You can keep a minimal PSTN line with no features, no long-distance charges, and so on for as little as $20 a month. For anyone who is in a situation where Enhanced 911 (E911) is critical (for example, someone with a chronic health condition), this approach is highly recommended. Prices can vary, so check with your local phone company by asking for the total monthly fee for a "bare bones" (no features, no long-distance) phone line. Be sure to ask whether the price you are quoted includes all taxes and fees.

Which Service Should I Choose?

Now that you are familiar with some of the factors to consider, read the sections that follow to see how you can make an informed decision.

Looking at Total Costs

Costs are a little tricky because if you are not careful, you might end up in a worse financial position. The first thing to do is figure out your average long-distance costs. Who are you calling and where are they: regional, national, or international? If you are making a lot of international calls, VoIP might or might not be the answer, so check the rates from the various providers.

The second thing to consider in the cost is whether you already have high-speed Internet. If not, you are looking at $40–$50 for a broadband connection in addition to the $20–$30 that you will be charged for the VoIP service. This might not be all bad, because you can use your high-speed broadband connection for lots of things, not just VoIP service.

Finally, you need to decide how extensively you plan to use VoIP service(s). For example, if you decide to keep your PSTN line, you still need to pay for that, too. It might be helpful to write down your total costs in a table to compare your options. Start with what your current phone service costs per month, as sketched out in Table 7-1.

Table 7-1   Starting Services Summary

	Monthly	Long-Distance	Extras	Total
Primary PSTN Line	$40	$60	—	$100
Additional PSTN Line	$30	$10	—	$40
Broadband Cable/DSL	$40	—	—	$40
Cable VoIP Line	—	—	—	—
Internet VoIP Line	—	—	—	—
VoIP Chat Service	—	—	—	—
				$180

In this example, suppose that we started with a PSTN line that costs about $40 per month, and we spend on average $60 a month on long-distance. We also have a second PSTN line with more-basic services for $30 a month, and spend about $10 in long-distance on that line. Finally, we have a broadband connection for $40, for a total monthly bill of $180.

Now let's look at a few examples of how we can potentially reduce expenses in our monthly telephone costs. In the first alternative, shown in Table 7-2, we drop the second PSTN line, add an Internet VoIP line, and use that VoIP line primarily for our long-distance calls. This could bring our monthly costs down to about $115.

Table 7-2   Alternative 1: Keep a Basic PSTN Line and Add a VoIP Line for Long-Distance

	Monthly	Long-Distance	Extras	Total
Primary PSTN Line	$40	$10	—	$50
Additional PSTN Line	—	—	—	—
Broadband Cable/DSL	$40	—	—	$40
Cable VoIP Line	—	—	—	—
Internet VoIP Line	$25	Unlimited	—	$25
VoIP Chat Service	—	—	—	—
				$115

Depending on the current PSTN provider and choice of VoIP provider, a few differ-ences in features or service can exist when moving to a lower-priced VoIP package. Check with your providers for details.

Let's look at a second example. This time we decide to replace our two PSTN lines with a combina-tion of a cable VoIP line (such as Time Warner Cable Digital Phone Service) and an Internet VoIP line (such as Verizon Voicewing service). Table 7-3 shows the results.

Table 7-3   Alternative 2: Replace PSTN Lines with VoIP Lines

	Monthly	Long-Distance	Extras	Total
Primary PSTN Line	—	—	—	—
Additional PSTN Line	—	—	—	—
Broadband Cable/DSL	$40	—	—	$40
Cable VoIP Line	$40	Unlimited	—	$40
Internet VoIP Line	$30	Unlimited	—	$30
VoIP Chat Service	—	—	—	—
				$110

In this example, both VoIP lines have unlimited long-distance (within the United States), so our two lines end up costing a total of about $110.

 Sometimes you get what you pay for. Keep in mind that in the example just presented, both VoIP service lines depend on your broadband Internet connection. Lose that and you also lose both phone services. So while it's cheaper to have two VoIP lines than it is to keep a PSTN line and add a VoIP line, it could also be less reliable.

As a third example, because of the recent competition for your local phone services, you can often "renegotiate" your local phone package with your current provider. You might obtain a plan that's similar to a VoIP plan, with unlimited long-distance and lots of features, for a bit more money than you are paying for your current PSTN service. So let's assume you still drop the second PSTN line and replace that with a VoIP line, as summarized in Table 7-4.

Table 7-4   Alternative 3: Update the PSTN Plan and Add an Internet VoIP Line

	Monthly	Long-Distance	Extras	Total
Primary PSTN Line	$50	Unlimited	—	$50
Additional PSTN Line	—	—	—	—
Broadband Cable/DSL	$40	—	—	$40
Cable VoIP Line	—	—	—	—
Internet VoIP Line	$25	Unlimited	$5 (virual number)	$30
VoIP Chat Service	—	—	—	—
				$120

In Alternative 3 in Table 7-4, we now have a PSTN line for about $50 a month and a VoIP line as our second line for about $25 a month, both with unlimited national long-distance. Suppose for kicks that we also obtain a virtual number for our VoIP line so that we can save Grandma some long-distance costs whenever she calls us. This usually costs about $5 extra, bringing our total for this example to $120.

 Be sure to find out whether the VoIP provider has a service clause that locks you into a contract (usually for a year). If you cancel and you have not reached the end of the contract, you could face a hefty termination fee.

For all three examples, we saved $700–$800 a year in telephone costs. That's some pretty serious cash. These are just a couple of scenarios, and you (of course) must map out your costs and needs to see whether these alternatives will benefit your situation.

If you didn't already have a broadband Internet connection service, you can see that it costs $40–$50 a month. So if you have to add both this and the VoIP service, it might not immediately save you money. It will save many people money, but you need to analyze your options before making a decision.

You should also consider the following other factors:

- International calls

- Installation/activation costs

If you make a significant number of international calls, you should research which type of service will be best for you from a cost standpoint. A VoIP chat service will most likely be the best option.

Finally, make sure that you understand whether you will incur activation costs or one-time equipment costs to install the service you are considering.

Is It Reliable Enough?

We mention some of the voice quality issues inherent with VoIP in Chapter 4, so we won't go too deep into them here. We do talk a bit about what voice quality means when deciding whether to get VoIP and how you will use it.

Before signing up for VoIP, think about how you will use it. Do you plan to use it primarily for free long-distance with friends and family or for business? If you plan on using it for business, can you (or more importantly, the people you talk to) tolerate a bit of lost audio or a dropped call occasionally? In most cases, the quality with VoIP will be just fine, but in some instances (or occupations), even minor voice quality issues are not acceptable.

Does It Have the Features You Need?

One of the nice things about VoIP is that you get a bunch of features, usually for free. Call waiting, call forwarding, three-way calling, caller ID, voice mail, and call transfers are examples of these features. Whether these are important to you might factor into your cost assessment, as sketched out in Tables 7-1 through 7-4. For example, if you have call waiting and call forwarding with your traditional phone service, you are probably paying for it.

In general, VoIP services include quite a few features. PSTN services typically charge premiums for additional features; however, this is quickly changing. Because of the competition for your local phone service, many more features are now being offered even in PSTN services as part of the base rate.

However, it's a good idea to compare not only the monthly rates for service but also the list of features included versus those that cost extra. Make sure to tally up your total costs, including feature premiums.

Are Specialized Devices Supported?

Besides phones, other devices sometimes need to be plugged into a phone line. Consider the following examples:

- Fax machines

- Satellite TV and/or TiVo receivers

- Home alarm systems with remote monitoring

- TTY/TTD equipment

Because VoIP services can use existing phone handsets, and are simply converting analog signals to digital VoIP for transmission across the Internet, most devices that work with a PSTN line should also work with a VoIP line.

However, we highly recommended that you contact your VoIP provider to understand whether its service supports the specialized devices you need. Fax machines and satellite/TiVo receivers are most likely supported pretty well by VoIP services.

For home alarm systems that currently use your PSTN line for remote monitoring, we recommend discussing the potential impacts of switching such a system to a VoIP line with your alarm system company.

For TTY/TTD and other types of specialized equipment that provides telephone system accessibility for persons with disabilities, again we recommended that you discuss any impacts with your potential VoIP service provider and makers of the TTY/TTD equipment prior to switching them from a PSTN service.

Revisiting Safety and 911

Do we need to mention this again? Yes we do. Without going into detail again, just make sure that you know the limitations of 911 service with your VoIP service. All VoIP providers in the United States are required to get your written consent regarding 911 capabilities, and most providers post these capabilities on their websites.

You can also review this FCC fact sheet on VoIP and 911 service:

http://www.fcc.gov/cgb/consumerfacts/voip911.pdf

Comparing Plans

There are a couple of good resources available online for comparing different plans. First, consider OrderVoIP.com:

http://www.ordervoip.com

On this site, you can find a good comparison of the major VoIP plans (see Figure 7-1) by clicking **Services**.

Figure 7-1   OrderVoIP.com Comparison Chart

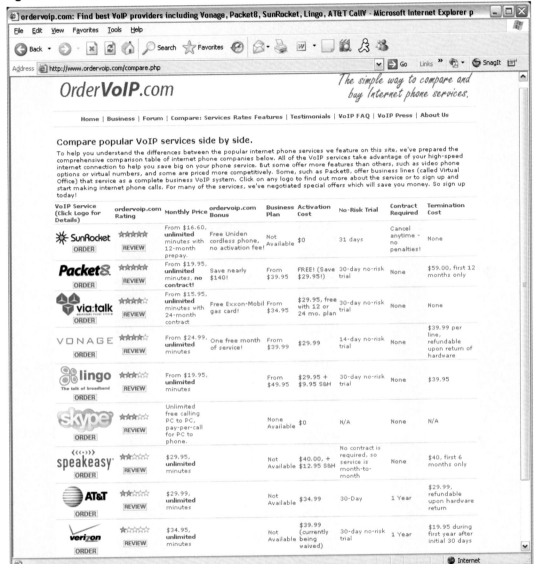

By clicking **Features**, you can compare the monthly costs and startup costs, and see some reviews by users of the different services. This gives a pretty high-level view, but it's a good place to start. You can also get a side-by-side summary of the features that the different services offer as well, as shown in Figure 7-2.

Figure 7-2   OrderVoIP.com Feature Summary Comparison

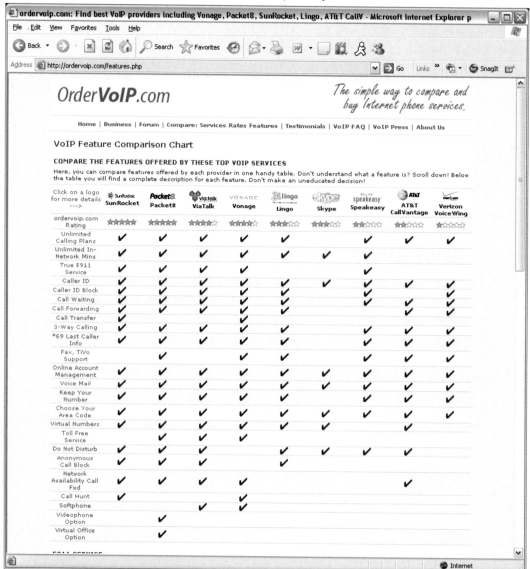

Another comparison site is VoipReview.org:

> http://www.voipreview.org

This site lets you type in your street address and zip code and tailor the search to the types of services that you are interested in. The search is narrowed to only those services that are available in your area. Figure 7-3 shows a sample search result.

Figure 7-3   VoipReview.org Search Results for Comparing VoIP Plans in Your Area

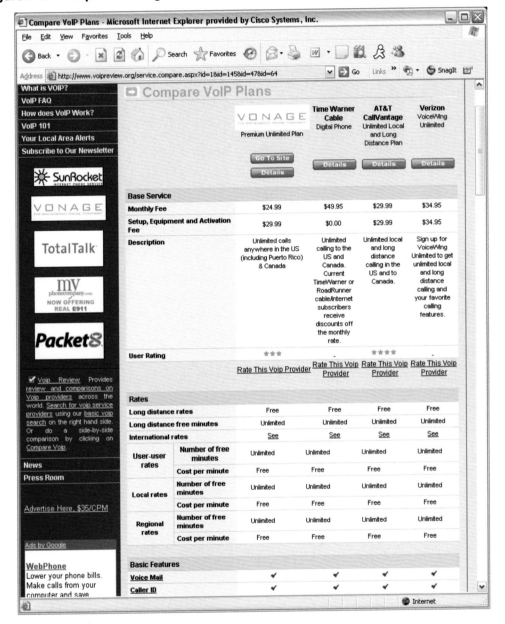

Using this site, you can again compare monthly costs, features, and so on to find a plan that's best for you.

Note In general, cable VoIP services are the only ones that are limited by where you are located. Internet VoIP services and VoIP chat services do not depend on the location of your home, so they are generally all available to you no matter where you live, assuming that you have access to high-speed Internet.

Summary

You should consider several factors when deciding which VoIP service(s) meet your needs. Hopefully this chapter has been useful in providing some useful decision criteria.

The quality of VoIP services depends on your specific broadband service provider and VoIP service provider. The best sources of information on which service works well in your area are often neighbors, friends, family, and coworkers who might already have different types of broadband services and VoIP services. Ask around and see what people think. You can also review the following online forums, which discuss and rate experiences:

- http://www.broadbandreports.com
- http://www.whichvoip.com
- http://compnetworking.about.com/od/voipvoiceoverip/

As a final note, Figure 7-4 is a flow chart that takes into consideration many of the points summarized within this chapter and previous chapters. It might not work perfectly for everyone, but it should give you a pretty good idea of whether VoIP is right for you, and if so, how much VoIP (an extra line or a complete swap-out) is appropriate.

Figure 7-4   Broadband Phone Service Flow Chart

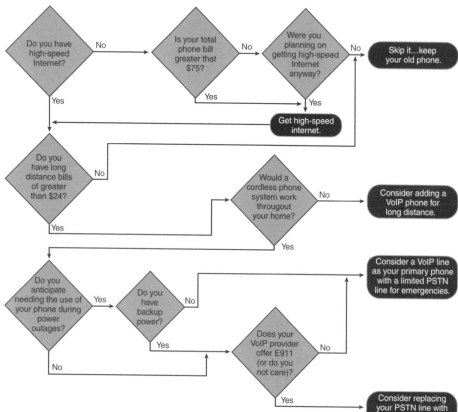

CHAPTER 8

Selecting VoIP Equipment

Now that you have a plan (or two) in mind, we take a look at the equipment required for each type of service. Cable VoIP and Internet VoIP services are similar, while VoIP chat service is quite different.

Cable VoIP Service Equipment

Cable VoIP services require a terminal adapter to convert the phone handsets in your home to VoIP. The terminal adapter function is often incorporated directly into the cable modem that's given to you by your broadband cable provider. Figure 8-1 shows examples of commonly used cable modems with integrated VoIP terminal adapters.

Figure 8-1   Integrated Cable Modem/VoIP Terminal Adapters

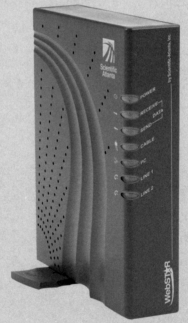

Motorola SBV4200   **Scientific Atlanta WebStar DPX2203**

When you sign up for the service (with your cable provider), you typically schedule an installation appointment, and the provider usually swaps out the cable modem you have (which is Internet only) with a dual-function cable modem/VoIP terminal adapter. This new VoIP-enabled cable modem fits into your home network, as shown in Figure 8-2.

Figure 8-2   Cable VoIP Equipment Setup

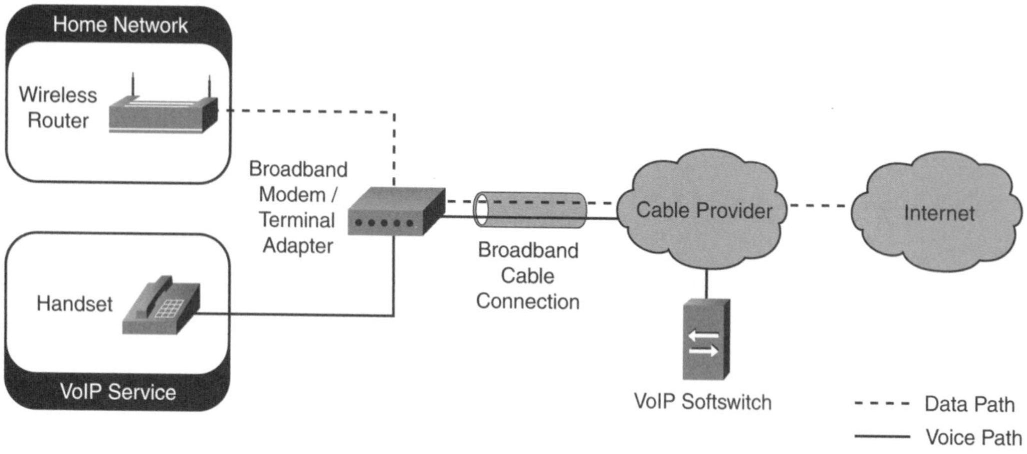

You don't have many options with this type of service. The equipment is generally chosen by your cable provider. But the key thing to understand is that the VoIP service is separate from your home network. You also typically have a wired or wireless router connected to the cable modem/VoIP terminal adapter that is providing your home network.

Chapter 11, "Making VoIP Accessible Throughout Your Home," discusses how this service integrates with your home phones and house telephone wiring.

Internet VoIP Service Equipment

Internet VoIP services are similar to cable VoIP services, and Internet VoIP also requires a terminal adapter. In this case, though, you have several equipment options.

When you sign up for the service (either online with the provider itself or at your favorite electronics retailer), you typically receive the terminal adapter for self-installation. It's easy, so don't panic. We step through the process in Chapter 10, "Connecting the VoIP Equipment," and we show you how to integrate the adapter with your home phones and house wiring in Chapter 11.

Choosing a Terminal Adapter

The primary decision to be made is whether to go with a stand-alone terminal adapter or an integrated router/terminal adapter. Stand-alone terminal adapters provide only the VoIP conversion of your phone handsets, and are a separate device from your home network router. Figure 8-3 shows a commonly used stand-alone terminal adapter.

Figure 8-3   Stand-alone VoIP Terminal Adapter

Linksys PAP2

Stand-alone terminal adapters connect to your home network by plugging them into the wired or wireless router that provides your home network. Figure 8-4 shows the setup for this option.

Figure 8-4   Internet VoIP Equipment Setup—Stand-alone

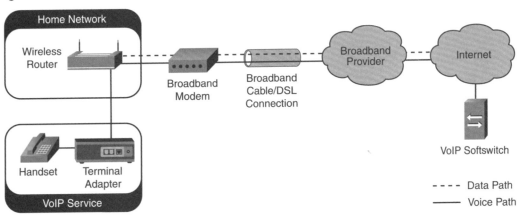

Another possibility is to have the VoIP terminal adapter integrated into a wired or wireless home network router. Figure 8-5 shows some commonly used products with integrated router/terminal adapters.

Figure 8-5   Integrated Wireless Router/VoIP Terminal Adapters

Linksys WRT54GP2

Linksys WRTP54G

With the integrated router/terminal adapter, the VoIP terminal adapter also provides your home network (Internet access). The router simply plugs into your broadband cable or digital subscriber line (DSL) modem, and then you connect a phone handset to the router/terminal adapter for the VoIP service. Figure 8-6 shows the integrated option.

Figure 8-6   Internet VoIP Equipment Setup—Integrated

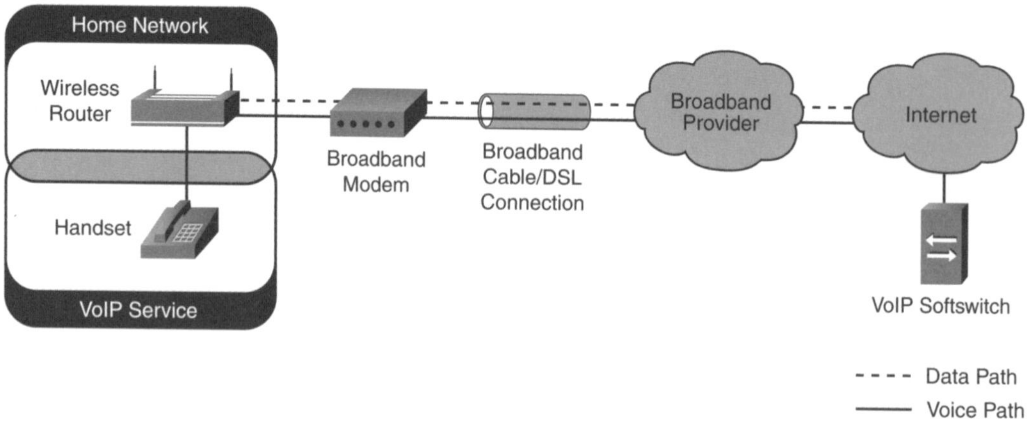

So which option should you choose? We recommend the stand-alone terminal adapter. While it requires an additional box that sits in your home alongside your wired or wireless network router, it also allows the two functions (home network and VoIP service) to be separated into two different boxes. That way, if you want to upgrade your home wireless network to a newer, faster standard, for example, you can do so without disrupting your VoIP service. Similarly, if you decide to switch VoIP providers, you can do so without disrupting your home network. If you choose an integrated router/terminal adapter, your home network and VoIP services are provided by a single device. So if you should decide to switch VoIP services, you could disrupt your home network.

What Do the Internet VoIP Providers Offer?

When selecting what type of terminal adapter to use, it is also important to see what your provider offers. The terminal adapter is usually tied to a particular provider, much like a cell phone you buy is tied to a specific mobile phone service provider.

Check the VoIP provider's website to see what types of stand-alone terminal adapters and integrated router/terminal adapter options it supports. VoIP providers commonly offer a stand-alone terminal adapter for free with activation, or you can purchase it for a small fee and a rebate often makes it free. Integrated router/terminal adapters usually cost more (you are paying for the router that provides your home network).

 Some VoIP providers require a service agreement of a year or more. If you terminate service, they might charge you a termination fee. Be sure to read the fine print!

If the service you choose does not offer a stand-alone terminal adapter option, you can still use that service as if it does. Figure 8-7 shows this option.

Figure 8-7   Internet VoIP Equipment Setup: Dual Routers

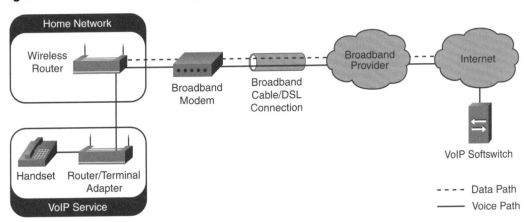

In this case, we do not disrupt the wireless router that is providing our home network, but instead we connect the router/terminal adapter from our provider behind the wireless router, essentially letting it act only as a terminal adapter.

Caution If the router/terminal adapter has wireless capability built in and you only want to use it for a terminal adapter, you must turn off the wireless function; otherwise, your home network will have a security hole.

VoIP Chat Service Equipment

VoIP chat services use your computer as the terminal adapter and possibly the phone handset as well. No additional equipment is required, except perhaps a good headset. Chapter 15, "VoIP Chat Services," and Chapter 16, "Using Skype and Google Talk," discuss the VoIP chat service requirements in further detail.

Summary

You must understand the type of equipment required to properly connect to the broadband phone service you have chosen.

Cable VoIP services are typically integrated directly into the cable modem by your provider. Internet VoIP services preferably have a stand-alone terminal adapter that you can connect to your home network wireless router. VoIP chat services use your computer as the terminal adapter and only require a high-speed Internet connection and some software.

Chapters 10 through 13 discuss how to connect the terminal adapter to your home network, how to integrate a VoIP service into your phone handsets and house wiring, and how to troubleshoot if problems occur.

Note In this chapter and other chapters, we show a wireless router for the home network router. A wireless router is not required and certainly a wired router could be used. However, wireless routers offer a great deal of flexibility, and we highly recommend them for home networks.

 # From the Geek Squad Files

The biggest thing to remember about choosing an Internet telephony provider is that unlike the regular phone company, you have lots of choices. Shop around for the best deal, and occasionally check back and see whether even better deals are available. Use your consumer power. Consider the following things:

- **Compatible systems**—All the standard Internet telephony providers to systems are interoperable with each other (meaning that you can call from any one of them to any of the others), the regular phone system, and the cellular phone system. Just because your friends and family use one type of provider does not mean that you have to use the same one.

- **Bundled services**—Some service providers offer only one type of service (for example, only Internet phone service), whereas others offer the entire enchilada (cable TV, Internet access, and Internet phone service). The service providers who offer more than one service can often give you a price break if you buy everything from them. In addition, you only have one provider to call and complain to if you have a problem. The downside to this could be that you also get bundled quality and customer service. Again, shop around.

- **Switching providers**—While number portability exists between the public switched telephone network (PSTN) and the digital providers, this might not be the case among Internet phone providers. This might not be a big deal if you use your phone mostly for outgoing free long-distance calls, but it could be a minor annoyance if you get a lot of incoming calls because you will have to tell everyone who calls you the new number if you switch providers. It's not a huge deal, but something to consider.

- **Quality levels**—If you get Internet phone service from a local cable provider, it probably provides dedicated bandwidth for your phone service. This means that your voice quality will not be affected if you send or receive large e-mail attachments while talking. If you subscribe to a third-party service (one that uses your regular high-speed Internet connection), your quality can be affected by your Internet use. Typically the service provided by the cable company costs more, but the quality is better and more consistent.

- **Emergency services**—Some providers offer Enhanced 911 (E911) service at this time. This could be an important consideration when choosing a service. You can usually find what type of emergency service each provider offers on its website (usually in the FAQ section of the site).

- **Other services**—At this time, most of the Internet phone services do not (officially) support things like fax lines or other analog services, so if you need any of these, you must keep an analog (regular phone) line in the house. We have seen fax machines that work over digital phone lines, but they are not "officially supported" by the carriers.

PART III
Going VoIP at Home

Part III is where the book changes from an "inform the consumer" book to a "how-to" book. If you are staring blankly at a bunch of equipment and a tangle of cables, this section is for you.

Chapter 10, "Connecting the VoIP Equipment," provides a detailed description of how to set up your VoIP system by yourself. Even if your VoIP provider installed the equipment for you, this chapter should be useful in the event that you decide to change things to better suit your usage or living arrangements.

Chapter 11, "Making VoIP Accessible Throughout Your Home," dives a little deeper into the setup, taking you from just the basics of getting dial tone to extending your VoIP system throughout your house. Here we discuss using cordless phones systems (which can cause quality issues if not connected properly), using two line phones, and even using your existing phone wiring for VoIP.

Chapter 12, "Using Wireless Networks to Extend VoIP," discusses yet another extension method. This is not particularly common, but it's not that difficult to accomplish. We've separated this topic as a separate chapter because you have additional considerations, including equipment purchases.

We end this part of the book with a chapter on troubleshooting. We've tried hard to make sure that everything will work for you, but stuff happens. Rather than giving you a catalog of problems and fixes, we have written this chapter to help you classify the trouble. VoIP service can run over multiple systems (for example, your service could run over the VoIP equipment, your home network, your broadband provider's network, and then the VoIP providers network). Given all this, it's important to know how to isolate issues to avoid frustration.

When used properly, Internet phone services can offer significant advantages. As we said in the introduction, our aim for this book is to enable our readers to make good choices.

CHAPTER 10

Connecting the VoIP Equipment

This chapter discusses how to connect VoIP service in your home. You have several different possibilities. We don't go through all of them, but spend some time on a couple of the most common types.

Starting Point

As a starting point (and so we can keep this book to a reasonable length), we need to make the following assumptions:

- You already have a high-speed broadband Internet service installed and working.

- The broadband service has a minimum of 128 kbps uplink bandwidth (from your home to the broadband provider), and preferably higher (such as 256 or 284 kbps). Most broadband providers have some sort of "speed test" on their Internet sites, or you can use the following link: http://www.broadbandreports.com/stest.

- The home network should be set up to assign dynamic IP addresses (this is the default for Linksys home routers).

- You have a home network set up, most likely using a home router (either wired or wireless). If you need help with this, see our other book, *Home Networking Simplified* (by Cisco Press).

Okay, now that our shameless plug is out of the way, let's move on to setting up the different types of VoIP services.

 Note: If your home network is set up with static IP addresses (you probably know if it is), you need to manually configure the terminal adapter to use static IP addressing. See the addendum section at the end of this chapter if you need to perform such a manual configuration. The example shown is for a Linksys PAP2 router. If your network uses DHCP to assign addresses (the most common case), keep going; you don't need to read the addendum.

Connecting Cable VoIP Service

If you decide to go with a cable VoIP service, in most cases, you can call your cable TV company and set up a professional installation.

When you call, you need to specify whether you want to replace your existing phone (that is, have the provider rewire your house so that all your phones are on the new digital system) or whether you want a single line (which means that you will have one phone jack out of the back of your modem/terminal adapter for digital phone service and the rest of your phones stay as they were). The provider might assume full replacement, so make sure that you specify what you want. If you request a full replacement, the provider will ask you whether you want to keep your existing phone number (refer to Chapter 3, "Advantages of Broadband Phone Services," and read the discussion on Local Number Portability) or acquire a new one. If you are replacing your public switched telephone network (PSTN) number, you should probably keep your existing number unless, of course, you are in a witness protection program or fleeing telemarketers, in which case you might want to select a new number.

By the way, if you select a new number for your VoIP service, you might have just inadvertently opened your household to telemarketers. If you had your previous number registered for telemarketers not to call you, make sure to register your new number as well. This can be done in about 5 minutes (in the United States) by visiting http://www.donotcall.gov.

To install a cable VoIP service, a technician will likely perform the following steps to install your service (this example assumes that the service is replacing a primary PSTN line). Refer to Figure 10-1 during the following setup:

Step 1. Disconnect the PSTN telephone wires at the junction box outside your home. This is necessary to remove the PSTN service and substitute cable VoIP service.

If you want to keep a single PSTN line for emergency backup, you need to let the cable installer know before he begins. If you do not tell the installer, he will likely take out all the PSTN lines to your house.

Step 2. Replace your existing Internet-only cable modem (or install a new one) with a new cable modem that also acts as a VoIP terminal adapter.

Step 3. Reconnect your home network to the new cable modem/terminal adapter for Internet service.

Step 4. Connect a telephone handset with an RJ11 phone cable directly to the cable modem/terminal adapter.

Step 5. Optionally, the installer might connect another RJ11 phone cable to a wall outlet in your house. This is discussed further in Chapter 11, "Making VoIP Accessible Throughout Your Home."

Figure 10-1   Cable VoIP Setup

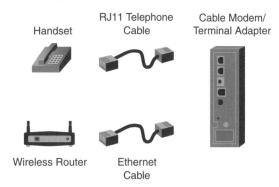

When the cable modem/terminal adapter is powered on, it establishes communication with the cable system and then to the high-speed broadband Internet system. When Internet connectivity is up and running, the VoIP terminal adapter (in this case, it's inside the cable modem) registers with the cable VoIP system, and the VoIP phone service is activated.

Several different manufacturers provide cable modems with integrated terminal adapters (including Scientific Atlanta, Motorola, and others). Each one varies, but you might find an LED on the front of the device marked "Phone" or "VoIP." If present, this LED should illuminate, indicating that the terminal adapter has successfully registered with the VoIP provider system. If no LED exists on the particular cable modem/terminal adapter, ask the installer if there is another way to tell whether the VoIP service is working.

The next step would be to make a test call (described in the section "Making a Test Call," later in this chapter).

Connecting Internet VoIP Service

If you decide to go with an Internet VoIP service, in most cases, it is installed as an addition to your PSTN service. You usually install an Internet VoIP service yourself. Don't worry—it's easy. The sections that follow show you how.

Signing Up for Service

The first step is to sign up for the service. This is usually done at the time you purchase a terminal adapter at your favorite electronics store (for example, Best Buy, Circuit City, and so on). You can also order the service online, in which case the terminal adapter is mailed to you.

Terminal adapters for some major services (including Vonage and AT&T CallVantage) are sold in retail stores. Others, including Verizon Voicewing, Packet8, and so on, are sold online through the provider's website (see Chapter 6, "Inventory of Broadband Phone Services") or a customer service number. Third-party online stores, such as Amazon.com, are also an option for some services. Most terminal adapters are preconfigured for the service they are sold for, which means that (much like a cell phone) they usually only work with the service for which you purchase them. There are exceptions to this, so make sure that you read the box before you buy the gear.

When you decide on a VoIP service provider, pick up a terminal adapter (TA) for that service and then register that TA with the service. This can often be done in the store with the assistance of a salesperson, or after you get home, you can register it online through the provider's website.

To register, you must provide your name, address, billing information, and the MAC address of the terminal adapter. (The address is on the box and on a label on the back or bottom of the terminal adapter.) The MAC address is usually written as a combination of twelve digits and letters (technically, hexadecimal numbers) with dashes, such as "A0-34-1D-66-EF-28." You must correctly identify the MAC address, because it is the single piece of information that identifies your terminal adapter to the VoIP service provider over the Internet.

 Note: To find out more about MAC addresses, what they are, and what they are used for, pick up a copy of our other book, *Home Networking Simplified* (by Cisco Press).

At this point, you also need to select a service plan. Most providers offer a basic service for a low price that has a limited number of minutes (such as 500) included, and a premium service for a few more dollars per month that has unlimited minutes. Choose which is right for you, but we recommend the premium service. After all, you are going to save a boatload on long-distance charges, so why be bothered with counting your minutes?

You also need to choose a phone number. In many cases, you have the option of keeping your existing PSTN number (assuming that you are replacing it) or selecting a new one. As we describe in Chapter 3, with Internet VoIP services, you typically have the option of choosing a phone number in almost any area code you want, and you can pick multiple additional virtual numbers as well (these cost extra, usually about $5 a month). Choose whichever phone number(s) fits your situation. The VoIP provider now links those numbers to your terminal adapter in its database.

After signing up, you can go home and start connecting your service. Optionally, many retail stores provide an option for you to have a professional installation as well, usually at an additional cost to you.

Installing a Stand-alone Terminal Adapter

In Chapter 8, "Selecting VoIP Equipment," we talk about two different options for terminal adapters: stand-alone and integrated. This section discusses how to install a stand-alone TA. Integrated router/terminal adapters are covered in the following section.

Perform the following steps to install your stand-alone terminal adapter (such as the Linksys PAP2). Refer to Figure 10-2 during the following setup:

Step 1.   Using an Ethernet cable, connect the terminal adapter (the port marked "Ethernet") to an open-wired switch port (usually marked "1," "2," "3," or "4") on the existing home router that provides your home network. If you do not have a router and are using an integrated broadband modem/router, connect the terminal adapter directly to an Ethernet port on the modem/router.

Step 2. Connect a telephone handset with a regular phone cable (RJ11) directly to the terminal adapter, in the port marked "Phone 1."

Step 3. Plug the terminal adapter's power cord into a wall outlet.

Step 4. Optionally, connect another phone cable (RJ11) from the terminal adapter to a wall outlet in your house. This is discussed further in Chapter 11.

Figure 10-2   Internet VoIP Setup Using a Terminal Adapter (Linksys PAP2)

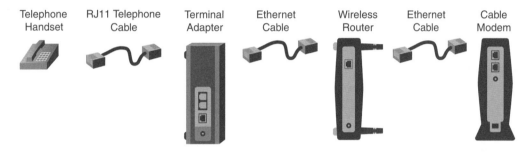

Telephone Handset   RJ11 Telephone Cable   Terminal Adapter   Ethernet Cable   Wireless Router   Ethernet Cable   Cable Modem

When the terminal adapter is powered on, it checks to see whether it can make a connection with your home network, and then registers with the VoIP system over the Internet. While this is taking place, you should see the LEDs on the TA illuminate. First, the "Power" LED blinks and then stays lit, indicating that the TA has finished booting up. Second, the "Ethernet" LED illuminates, telling you it has made a connection to the home network. Finally the "Phone 1" LED illuminates, indicating that the TA has successfully registered to the VoIP provider system, and the VoIP phone service is activated.

The next step would be to make a test call (described later in this chapter).

Installing an Integrated Router/Terminal Adapter

If you already have a home network with a router, and your VoIP provider only gives you the option of using an integrated router/terminal adapter, you can still install the VoIP service without disrupting your existing home network (and router). In this case, installing an integrated router/terminal adapter is similar to installing a stand-alone TA. Perform the following steps to install your integrated router/terminal adapter (such as the Linksys RTP300, WRTP54G, WRT54GP2, or RT41P2). Refer to Figure 10-3 during the following setup:

Step 1. Using an Ethernet cable, connect the router/terminal adapter (the port marked "Internet") to an open-wired switch port (usually marked "1," "2," "3," or "4") on your existing home router or wireless router that provides your home network.

Step 2. Connect a telephone handset with an RJ11 phone cable directly to the router/terminal adapter, in the port marked "Phone 1."

Step 3. Plug the router/terminal adapter's power cord into a wall outlet.

Step 4. Optionally, connect another phone cable (RJ11) from the router/terminal adapter to a wall outlet. This is discussed further in Chapter 11.

Figure 10-3   Internet VoIP Setup Using a Router/Terminal Adapter (Linksys RT41P2)

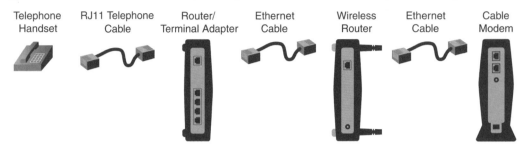

Because the integrated router/terminal adapter also contains a router function, you can plug it directly into your broadband modem, if you don't already have a home network router. As we mention in Chapter 8, we recommend using two separate devices for your home network router and terminal adapter. But if you don't already have a home network and the VoIP provider gives you an integrated router/terminal adapter, you can certainly take advantage of it. Figure 10-4 illustrates the installation setup in this case.

Figure 10-4   Setup Using a Wireless Router/Terminal Adapter (Linksys WRTP54G) Without a Separate Home Network Router

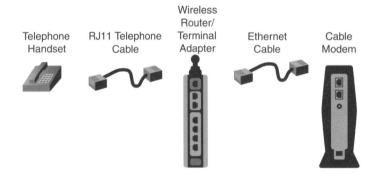

When the router/terminal adapter is powered on, it checks to see whether it can make a connection with your home network, and then registers with the VoIP system over the Internet. While this is taking place, you should see the LEDs on the TA illuminate. First, the "Power" LED blinks and then stays lit, indicating that the TA has finished booting up. Second, the "Ethernet" LED illuminates, telling you that it has made a connection to the home network. Finally the "Phone 1" LED illuminates, indicating that the TA has successfully registered to the VoIP provider system, and the VoIP phone service is activated.

Because the integrated equipment also has a built-in router, and potentially a built-in wireless access point, you might need to perform several other configuration steps. If it's a wired router, at a minimum, you need to change the administrative password. If it also contains a wireless access point, you should also disable the wireless function (assuming that you already have a wireless home router). If you leave the wireless access point enabled, as it comes "out of the box" from the manufacturer, it can be a security hole in your home network. We recommend that you read our other book, *Home Networking Simplified* (by Cisco Press), for more information on that subject.

The next step would be to make a test call (described later in this chapter).

Connecting VoIP Chat Service

Chapter 15, "VoIP Chat Services," and Chapter 16, "Using Skype and Google Talk," discuss VoIP chat service installation and use in greater detail.

Making a Test Call

Now that you have your VoIP service connected (whether cable VoIP or Internet VoIP), it's time to make a test call to see whether it works.

Let's start with just a handset connected directly to the terminal adapter to make sure that the VoIP service is working properly. Connect any of your existing handsets, preferably a simple corded PSTN handset—not cordless yet.

 Caution For phone handsets to work properly with a VoIP service, they should be set for tone dialing, not pulse dialing. A toggle switch is provided on the phone for this setting. If you still have a rotary phone that does not support tone dialing, it won't work with VoIP, and it's probably time for you to donate it to a museum anyway.

Pick up the handset receiver and check for a dial tone. If no dial tone exists, something has not occurred properly in connecting the VoIP service. Recheck that you followed the steps discussed earlier in this chapter, including the simple stuff like plugging in power cables. If you still have no dial tone, consult Chapter 13, "Troubleshooting: Can You Hear Me Now?"

If you hear a dial tone, try placing an outgoing call by dialing a known phone number you have access to, such as your PSTN phone line (assuming that you didn't just replace it), a cell phone, or a willing participant such as a friend or family member. You should hear the phone ringing, just as if you were using a PSTN phone. If it works (meaning that you can hear and be heard), your VoIP service is connected properly.

 This is a great time to ask the person you are calling whether he has Prince Albert in can.

Next, try placing an incoming call from your PSTN phone or a cell phone to the VoIP line. The VoIP line should ring. You can answer it, say thanks to your helper, and hang up the phone.

Congratulations, you just installed a VoIP phone line!

If you are unable to place or receive calls, recheck that you are dialing the correct numbers. If you picked a phone number in another area code, make sure you are using 10-digit dialing (in the United States), which includes the area code of the phone number you are dialing (usually no leading "1" is required, but check with your provider). If you still cannot place or receive calls, see Chapter 13.

911 or E911 Registration

After installing a VoIP service, whether cable VoIP or Internet VoIP, you must follow the instructions from the service provider on how to register your location for 911 and Enhanced 911 (E911) services.

This usually involves completing a registration form on your provider's website or over the phone if you signed up through a customer service representative. The provider then confirms your location with your local emergency service's Public Safety Answering Point (PSAP). The provider then notifies you that 911 and/or E911 services are established for your VoIP phone. Notification might be instant or later, through e-mail, letter, or other type of communication.

VERY IMPORTANT: **Some people have asked whether they should test their 911/E911 service by dialing 9-1-1. That's a tough question to answer. On one hand, it would be nice to know that the registration has been made correctly by the provider with your PSAP, and that the correct location information appears on the PSAP agent's computer screen. On the other hand, none of us want to add additional unnecessary call volume to the already hard-working folks at the PSAP.**

For those of us who have not had the need to use 911 emergency services, even from our PSTN phone, we take for granted that the PSAP folks have our location information correct in their database. But hypothetically, your PSAP might already have incorrect information, regardless of whether you install a VoIP service. However, switching to a VoIP provider does offer an additional opportunity for human error.

After much hand-wringing, we recommend that you ask your VoIP provider how it recommends you should validate 911/E911 registration. In addition, you might want to talk with someone in your community who is familiar with the PSAP operations in your area (for example, police, fire, and EMS personnel) for a recommendation.

Summary

Now that you have installed the VoIP service, made a test call to make sure that it is working, and completed the 911/E911 registration, you can move on to extending the service inside your house.

Addendum: Manually Configuring Terminal Adapters for Home Networks Using Static IP Addresses

We recommend that you use DHCP to assign IP addresses automatically in your home network. If your home network is set up with DHCP enabled (most are, unless you have a good reason not to), you can skip this section.

In the event that your home network is configured with static IP addresses (if you have set it up this way you would know it), the VoIP terminal adapter must be configured manually to work in your network. Follow these steps to do so (this example is for a Linksys PAP2 terminal adapter):

Step 1. Unplug the Ethernet cable from the TA (if one is plugged in) but leave the power cord plugged in (or plug it in if it's not already powered on).

Step 2. Plug a regular phone handset into the port marked "Phone 1."

Step 3. Pick up the handset and dial ****. You should hear a voice prompt telling you that you are in the configuration menu.

Step 4. Dial **101#** and then **0#** to disable DHCP. Press **1** when the voice prompt asks whether you want to save.

Step 5. Dial **111#** and then the IP address you want the TA to use, using the star (*) key as the "dot." For example, to assign 192.168.1.130, dial **192*168*1*130#**. Press **1** when the voice prompt asks whether you want to save.

Step 6. Dial **121#** and then the subnet mask you want the TA to use, using the * key as the "dot." For example, to assign 255.255.255.0, dial **255*255*255*0#**. Press **1** when the voice prompt asks whether you want to save.

Step 7. Dial **131#** and then the gateway IP address that you want the TA to use, using the * key as the "dot." For example, to assign 192.168.1.1, dial **192*168*1*1#**. Press **1** when the voice prompt asks whether you want to save.

Step 8. Dial **110#** to check the static IP address to make sure that you entered it correctly. Dial **120#** to check the subnet mask, and dial **130#** to check the gateway IP address. Go back to the appropriate step if you entered something incorrectly.

Step 9. Hang up the phone handset. Disconnect the power cord. Plug the Ethernet cable back into the terminal adapter and power it back on.

Check to make sure that the assigned static IP address works. After a few seconds of bootup, the LEDs marked "Power," "Ethernet," and "Phone1" should illuminate and stay lit. Pick up the phone handset and see whether you have a dial tone. Continue following the test procedures (or troubleshooting) in the appropriate previous section.

If you have a different terminal adapter than the example shown here, check the user guide that came with the adapter to determine how to manually configure it. In general, you must follow the steps to disable DHCP and set the IP address, subnet mask, and gateway IP address. If you set up your home network with static IP addressing (for whatever reason), you should already have some knowledge of IP addressing and how it works, and you should be familiar enough with the concepts here to set up your particular type of terminal adapter.

CHAPTER 11

Making VoIP Accessible Throughout Your Home

Now that we have connected a VoIP service and checked that it works, we can tackle the next piece of the puzzle. So far, we have a single corded phone handset connected to our terminal adapter.

This is typically not practical for most homes for the following reasons:

- It only allows you to place your phone wherever you have your Internet access (that is, alongside your broadband modem and wireless router that provide your home network), because this is where the terminal adapter has to be plugged in.

- A single phone handset is usually not enough for most households, particularly if you have teenagers who seem to use the phone most of the time.

This chapter looks at extending the VoIP service of your choice throughout your home to make it more accessible. You have two primary methods for doing so: using cordless telephones and using your existing home telephone wiring. We look at both in this chapter. Ultimately, you might end up using a combination of both methods.

Using Cordless Phones with VoIP

The simplest and most straightforward way to extend VoIP throughout your home is to take advantage of cordless phone systems. Connecting a cordless phone to your VoIP terminal adapter is easy, as Figure 11-1 illustrates.

Figure 11-1   Using a Cordless Phone with VoIP

Terminal	RJ11	5.8-GHz
Adapter	Telephone	Cordless
	Cable	Phone

Instead of connecting a corded phone handset, you simply connect the base of the cordless phone to the terminal adapter with a basic telephone cable (RJ11, the one with the narrow plug). That's it; you're set to go. This provides basic connectivity throughout your house. With extendable cordless phone systems, you can even add handsets. It might help to digress briefly on cordless phone system types so that you purchase the right one for your needs.

Remember that cordless phones might use the same frequency as your wireless router and could cause interference. Whichever one you have first (the phone or the router), be sure to purchase the other with a different frequency. For example, if you have an 802.11b/g wireless home network, it operates at 2.4 GHz, so you should buy cordless phones that operate at 5.8 GHz. The frequency is printed on the box of the phone and router.

Several different types of cordless phone systems exist, with many bells and whistles to consider. The following two questions are pertinent to the discussion in this chapter:

- How many phone lines do you plan to have coming into your house?

- How many handsets do you need to have access to the line(s)?

Cordless phone systems come in single-line and two-line designs (or even more). Two-line systems allow you to place and receive calls over two different lines using the same set of handsets. This can be handy if you have more than one phone line, for example, a public switched telephone network (PSTN) line and a VoIP line. We talk about this in the section "Home Wiring with Internet VoIP Service," later in this chapter, and the advantages of this approach then become apparent.

Extendable systems allow you to have a single cordless phone base connected to your terminal adapter and to have more than one handset to place throughout your house (usually up to four, but sometimes as many as eight).

Separate PSTN and VoIP Lines

Suppose that you decide to keep your PSTN service but add a VoIP service, perhaps as a second inexpensive phone line for a teenager. One approach you could take then would be to keep your existing PSTN phone handsets and purchase a cordless phone for your VoIP line, as shown in Figure 11-2.

In this example, you have separate handsets for each phone service. If you want to place a call using the PSTN (line 1), you must use the handset or cordless phone connected to that service. Similarly, you have to use the cordless phone connected to the VoIP service (line 2) if you want to use that line.

This can be effective if you have "zones" in your house that separate phone line use. For example, the PSTN phone could be used by the family downstairs, and the VoIP line can be used by teenagers upstairs.

Figure 11-2 Separate Handsets for PSTN and VoIP Lines

Internet
VoIP Line
Terminal
Adapter
RJ11
Telephone
Cable
5.8-GHz
Cordless
Phone
PSTN Line
Home Wall
Outlet
RJ11
Telephone
Cable
5.8-GHz
Cordless
Phone

Two-Line Cordless Phones

In situations where you are using VoIP service, perhaps as your primary long-distance calling service, and still using the PSTN service for all local calls, the separate PSTN and VoIP lines approach might not be practical. Hunting for the right cordless phone can be a chore, and people usually just make the call on the nearest handset, regardless of the costs involved. That quickly defeats your purpose.

So in cases where most people in your house use both lines, a two-line cordless phone system can be useful. Figure 11-3 shows an example, where we have a PSTN line (line 1) and an Internet VoIP service (line 2) both connected to a single cordless phone system.

Figure 11-3 Two-Line Handsets for PSTN and VoIP Lines

Internet
VoIP Line
Terminal
Adapter
Line 2
2-Line 5.8-GHz
Extendable Cordless
Phone System
PSTN Line
Home Wall
Outlet
Line 1

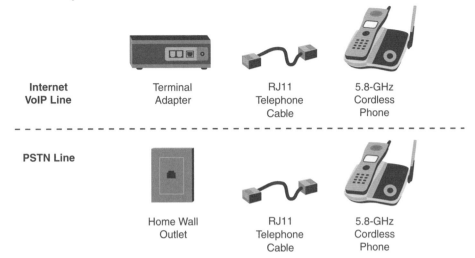

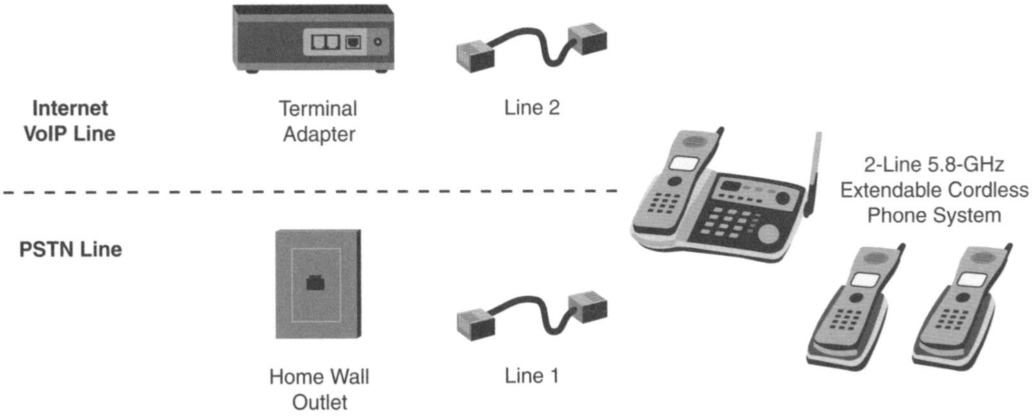

Now you can have both lines available on all the handsets in the house. You simply select Line 1 or Line 2 on the handset whenever you want to place a call. Incoming calls are identified by the handset as arriving on line 1 or line 2, complete with caller ID information as well. This is a practical approach, although two-line extendable cordless phone systems tend to be pricier than single-line systems.

By the way, this same approach can be used if you have replaced your PSTN line with a cable VoIP service (line 1) and also have an Internet VoIP service (line 2). In this case, you would have both VoIP terminal adapters connected to the input lines on the cordless phone system, as shown in Figure 11-4.

Figure 11-4   Two-Line Handsets for Two VoIP Lines

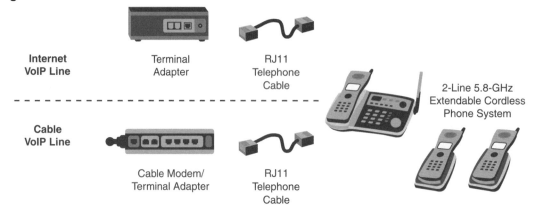

Remember that in this example, you have disconnected all PSTN access. As a result, both of your phone lines are being powered by the electricity in your home, so if you lose power, neither of your phones will work. Regarding this topic, be sure to read Chapter 4, "Knowing Your Limits."

That's it for cordless phones—pretty easy, no muss, no fuss. Next we look at an option that's a bit more difficult.

Using Your Home Telephone Wiring with VoIP

Another way to extend VoIP throughout your home is to take advantage of the existing telephone wiring in your home. It's not for the novice, and you should probably be a little comfortable with some basic wiring skills. If this intimidates you, ask a friend or family member for help, hire a professional, or stay with cordless.

If you want to pursue this option, we don't have enough room in this book to teach you everything, but what follows in the next few sections is an overview.

Introduction to Home Telephone Wiring

Before we begin, you need to have a basic level of understanding of how your home telephone wiring works. We have intentionally oversimplified it a little, but you can get the general idea.

Most modern homes are cabled with standard 4-wire telephone cabling, as shown in the left side of Figure 11-5.

Figure 11-5   4-Wire House Telephone Wiring

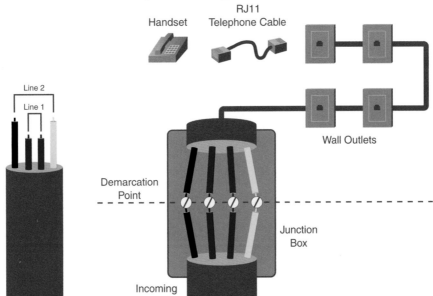

Telephone service only requires two wires, so if your home has the standard 4-wire cabling, you have the potential for two distinct phone lines in all the outlets in your home. If you ordered a second phone line from the PSTN provider in the past, the provider probably used the second wire pair to connect the second line throughout your home.

The primary phone line is carried on the red and green wire pair, while the second line is carried on the yellow and black wire pair. Keep in mind, home developers sometimes substitute the cheapest wiring they have, so don't be surprised if your home has a different color scheme. Some newer homes are even prewired with Category 5 (Cat5) cable.

The incoming line(s) from the PSTN are wired to a junction box at your house, possibly inside in the basement or attic. In newer homes, the junction box is often attached to the outside of the house for more convenient access by repair personnel. The junction box provides the following functions:

- It provides the "demarcation line" (also known as the *demarc*) that separates what the phone company owns and what you own. The phone company is responsible for the wiring from its central office to your junction box. You are responsible for the wiring from the junction box into your home.

- Because of the possibility of lightning strikes, a safety measure is provided in junction boxes to provide grounding so that lightning damage (usually) stops at the junction box and does not flow into your home.

 Note By the way, VoIP systems do not have their own lightning grounding protection because they operate on your broadband Internet connection. If your broadband is digital subscriber line (DSL), the PSTN wiring provides the grounding. If your broadband is cable, the cable TV system wiring provides the grounding protection. This is not to say that your home network or VoIP equipment is completely safe from lightning damage, but they are at least protected as well as your PSTN phone.

On the right side of Figure 11-5, you can see that the wiring in your home leaves the junction box and then makes its way to each wall outlet in your home. You might have thought that a separate wire exists from each outlet to the junction box. More than likely, the wiring is "daisy-chained" from outlet to outlet. This means that for each phone, one wire typically connects all the jacks in a single line (as opposed to each jack connecting directly to the junction box).

By connecting a standard phone cable (RJ11) to any outlet in your house, your handset can be connected to the PSTN through the junction box. What some folks do not realize is that this phone cable is only using half of the wires in the outlet. The other wires are there in the outlets but not used, unless you have your PSTN provider connect a second PSTN line.

That's it—Home Telephone Wiring 101.

Getting Access to Two Lines

So the next question is this: How *do* you connect a phone to that second set of wires in your home? You have a couple of possibilities.

First, you can visit your favorite electronics store and (for about $5) purchase a two-line wall plate, which has two physical jacks (holes for the phone plugs). This is shown in Figure 11-6.

Figure 11-6   Replace a Single-Jack Wall Plate with a Two-Line Wall Plate

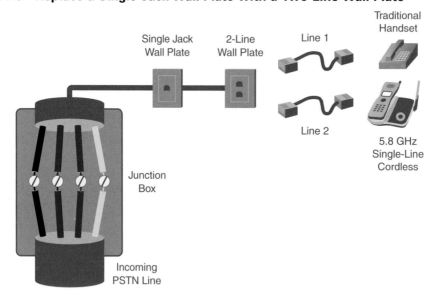

Replacing the wall plate involves removing the old plate, connecting the four wires to the new plate, and then attaching the plate cover. In doing so, remember to connect the correct wire pair to each of the two lines (the red/green pair to line 1 and the yellow/black pair to line 2).

VERY IMPORTANT: **Phone wiring can generally be touched without worry about electric shocks, although if someone calls, you might feel a tingling sensation. If you have a medical condition where even a low voltage could cause harm, do not attempt this repair.**

VERY IMPORTANT: **Never touch exposed wires or attempt to make repairs or changes to anything that is connected to a wall power outlet without first shutting the power off.**

Now you can plug two separate phones into the wall, one per line.

If you don't want to get into the phone wiring, you have another option. At the same electronics store, and for about the same cost, you can purchase a line splitter that plugs into your existing wall outlet, as shown in Figure 11-7.

Figure 11-7   Install a Two-Line External Splitter

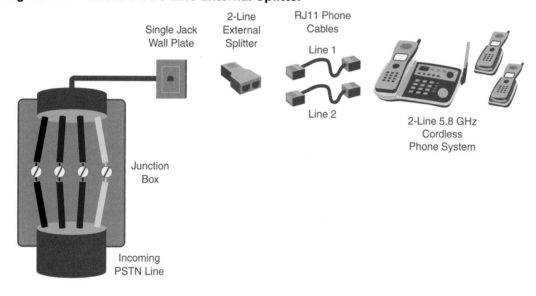

The splitter does the work of separating the four wires into their proper pairs and presents you with two convenient phone jacks for line 1 and 2. It's an easier option, but a bit more unsightly one.

For the sake of this example, we show a two-line cordless phone system being connected to the splitter. Note also that so far, we have not introduced VoIP into the picture. This short education about accessing the two phone lines in your house wiring is applicable even if you keep your PSTN lines. Next, we examine how VoIP fits into the picture.

Home Wiring with Cable VoIP Service

If you decide to go with a cable VoIP service, you will probably have a professional installation performed by the cable company, as we discuss in Chapter 10, "Connecting the VoIP Equipment."

But it is helpful to understand what the company typically does when it installs your service. As we discuss in Chapter 10, when you sign up for cable VoIP service, you must decide whether you want the service to replace your primary PSTN line or whether you want to have it installed as an additional line. If you don't specify an option, the cable company often assumes that you want your PSTN line replaced. Figure 11-8 shows the replacement of a PSTN line with a cable VoIP line.

Figure 11-8   How Cable VoIP Can Use Your House Wiring

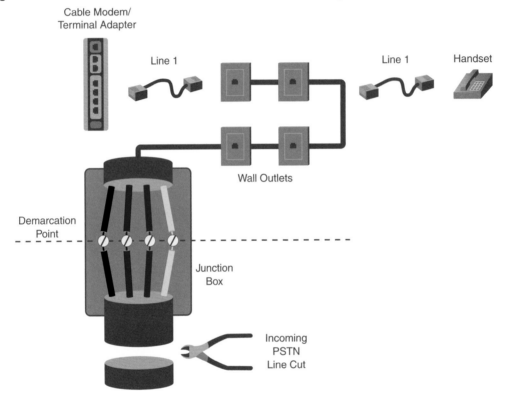

In this example, the PSTN line to your PSTN provider is severed, because the cable VoIP service is now your primary telephone line. In addition, the cable modem/terminal adapter is connected to one of the wall outlets in your home using an RJ11 phone cable.

 Do not plug a terminal adapter into the existing phone jack in your house unless you have disconnected the PSTN service. The voltage supplied by the PSTN can fry your terminal adapter.

At first look, this might be a bit confusing and you might ask, "Why does the terminal adapter need to receive a phone signal from my outlets?" The answer is that in this setup, the terminal adapter is using your home wiring to provide phone service to all the same outlets in your home that you used to have for PSTN phone access. So the connection between your cable modem/terminal adapter and the wall outlet is providing the same function as the PSTN line that used to connect to your junction box.

But instead of running a cable from the cable modem/terminal adapter back out to your junction box, it's more convenient to just use a nearby wall outlet to serve the same purpose.

Now any phone handset that you connect to any of your wall outlets can use the cable VoIP service as the phone line (line 1, in this example). Pretty neat!

Home Wiring with Internet VoIP Service

The last example we demonstrate is the case where you decide to keep your primary PSTN line and add an Internet VoIP line as a second line. You also decide that you want the VoIP service to use the line 2 wiring in your house so that you can connect a handset to line 2 using a wall outlet.

This is relatively straightforward. First, disconnect the second wire pair (yellow and black) at the PSTN junction box, leaving the primary wire pair (red and green) as it is, as illustrated in Figure 11-9.

Figure 11-9   How Internet VoIP Can Use Your House Wiring and Coexist with PSTN Service

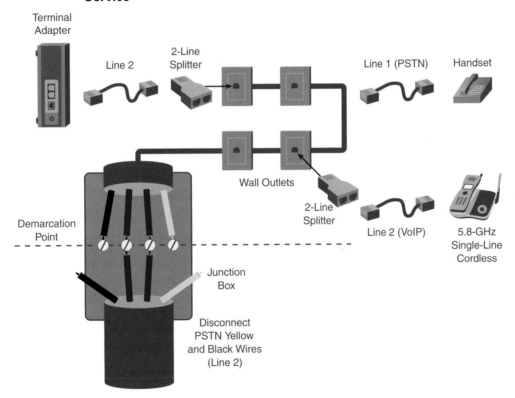

Tip If you are going to use your home telephone wiring with VoIP, you must disconnect the appropriate wiring at your PSTN junction box. If you are using just line 2 wiring for VoIP, disconnect the yellow and black wire pair. If you are replacing your PSTN service with VoIP, disconnect both pairs (all four wires) at the junction box.

Next, you can use line splitters that are plugged into the wall outlets to separate line 1 and line 2. The terminal adapter is connected to a nearby outlet (through a splitter) to line 2. Then you can use additional splitters wherever you like to connect a handset explicitly to line 2. Figure 11-9 shows a traditional handset connected to line 1 (PSTN service) and a cordless handset connected in a different room to line 2 (VoIP service).

This can be effective if you want to have certain outlets (that is, rooms) in your home connected to one type of service or the other—or potentially both.

Caution If you are planning to disconnect your PSTN service but keep your high-speed broadband DSL service, you might not be able to use your home wiring for VoIP. DSL uses the same wiring as the PSTN to bring Internet service to your home. Disconnecting the PSTN wiring at the junction box will obviously also disconnect your DSL service.

Issues with Multiple Handsets

You must consider a couple of issues when connecting multiple corded or cordless handsets to your VoIP service. The sections that follow describe these considerations in detail.

Overloading Your Terminal Adapter's Ringer Equivalence Number

The first issue to consider when connecting multiple handsets occurs when all the handsets are on hook and waiting for an incoming call. You probably did not realize it, but your current PSTN home phone line has a limit to how many phone handsets can be properly connected to it. This limit, called the Ringer Equivalence Number (REN), is related to the power supplied by the PSTN central office to make your phone handsets ring. Most modern PSTN circuits have a REN limit of five. Plugging in more than five handsets might prevent the phones from ringing properly.

With VoIP service, the terminal adapter (whether it's a cable VoIP service or Internet VoIP service) provides ringing to the handsets connected to it. Like a PSTN line, terminal adapters also have a REN limit. (The limit is usually five, but check the specific equipment for your service.)

Note Linksys terminal adapters, including stand-alone products such as the PAP2 and integrated router/terminal adapter products such as the RT41P2 and WRTP54G, all have REN limits of five. Unless you plan to connect more than 5 analog handsets or 20 or so cordless handset bases, overloading is generally not a concern.

You don't have to be overly concerned about exceeding the REN limit of your terminal adapter. Just don't attach a dozen analog handsets to a single VoIP line.

If you have many handsets connected and are concerned about overloading your terminal adapter, you can calculate your REN "load" by totaling the number of phone handsets connected to the same line and making sure that this number is less than the REN limit of the terminal adapter. As a rule, if a handset has its own power plug (such as a cordless handset), it usually has a low REN, probably 0.2. If a handset has no power plug, it most likely has a REN near 1.0. By the way, if you have an extendable cordless phone (where the base is connected to a phone outlet, but not each phone handset), you only count the base, not each handset, when calculating the REN.

Simultaneous Handsets Off Hook

When connecting multiple handsets, the next issue to consider is when more than one handset is off hook during a call. Similar to the way the PSTN provides power to ring phone handsets, it also provides the power to the handsets when they are off hook and someone is speaking. Have you ever had the experience where two or three people in your house pick up the phone to answer a call? The sound quality isn't as good as when only one person picks up the phone. In general, the sound quality of a call degrades as more handsets go off hook on the same call.

With VoIP services, the terminal adapter supplies the power (at least for handsets that do not have power of their own). Also similar to the PSTN, if more than one person has lifted the handset and is on the same call over the VoIP line, the sound quality can degrade.

In general, cordless handsets have less of an impact than analog handsets. Analog handsets typically have no separate power source and therefore depend on the terminal adapter for power. Cordless handsets have their own power supply and depend much less on the terminal adapter. By the way, for extendable cordless phones, the load on the terminal adapter is from the base only, so the load is the same regardless of whether one or multiple handsets are off hook (assuming that they connect through the same base unit).

Depending on the terminal adapter and how well the manufacturer designed it, the use of multiple handsets might work well, might provide degraded sound quality, or might have no sound. For example, we tested two different VoIP services, each with a different type of terminal adapter, and got differing results. For the first test, we used a cable VoIP service powered by an integrated cable modem/terminal adapter. We noticed no degradation in audio quality with up to three handsets simultaneously off hook during a call. For the second test, we used an Internet VoIP service powered by a stand-alone terminal adapter. The audio was fine with two handsets off hook but severely degraded when a third handset was lifted during a call.

The following are recommendations for dealing with this issue:

- If you typically have no more than one (or maybe two) persons on the same phone call in your house, you shouldn't have a problem.

- If you regularly have two or more persons talking on different handsets on the same call, you should invest in an extendable cordless phone system (see the section "Using Cordless Phones with VoIP," earlier in this chapter).

- Don't buy the cheapest terminal adapter you can find. Sometimes you get what you pay for. Consult your VoIP service provider to understand the terminal adapter options it offers and which ones might be better suited to handling multiple phone handsets.

Multiline VoIP Services

Earlier in this chapter, we discussed how to have multiple phone services (such as PSTN plus VoIP or cable VoIP plus Internet VoIP) integrated into your home telephone handsets and wiring. So why not just get two lines from the same VoIP service? The answer is that this might or might not be available and it might or might not be a good idea.

First we look at cable VoIP service. At the time this book was written, most cable providers offered only a single-line service but some had plans to offer second-line services in the near future. If available, two-line cable VoIP could be a practical service. It's helpful to understand how cable VoIP is handled by the cable system. Figure 11-10 shows an example of a two-line cable VoIP service combined with a broadband cable Internet service (note that this does not apply to DSL).

Figure 11-10 How Two-Line Cable VoIP Works

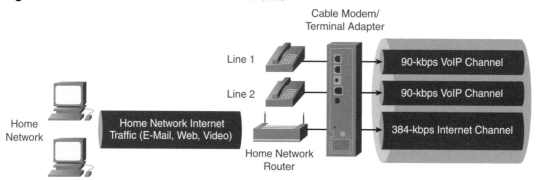

With cable VoIP, the cable modem/terminal adapter converts the analog conversations for line 1 and line 2 to VoIP packets. In this case, the VoIP packets are sent and received over the broadband link from your house to the broadband provider on dedicated "channels," which are separate from your broadband Internet service. Packets from computers on your home network (such as e-mail, web browsing, video, and so on) are sent and received from your home network router through the cable modem and on to the Internet.

Because the VoIP lines and Internet service are mapped to separate "channels" on the broadband link, you can have a high level of confidence that VoIP packets and home network packets will not interfere with each other and potentially result in call audio problems. Because of this, adding a second VoIP line to a cable VoIP service should be fairly reliable, regardless of the speed of your broadband Internet service.

Next we compare this with having a two-line Internet VoIP service. Figure 11-11 shows an example of a two-line Internet VoIP service combined with a broadband Internet service (this model applies to both broadband cable and DSL service).

Figure 11-11 How Two-Line Internet VoIP Works

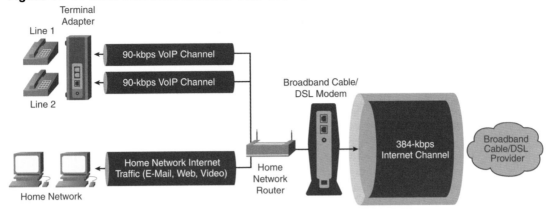

With Internet VoIP, the terminal adapter converts the analog conversations from line 1 and line 2 to VoIP packets, just like cable VoIP. In this case, though, the VoIP packets are sent and received over the broadband link from your house to the broadband provider on the same "channel" as your broadband Internet service. Packets from computers on your home network are sent and received from your home network router through the broadband modem and on to the Internet, mixed with VoIP packets.

Because the VoIP lines and Internet service are not mapped to separate "channels" on the broadband link, you can't always have a high level of confidence that VoIP packets and home network packets will not interfere with each other and potentially result in call audio problems. Because of this, adding a second VoIP line to an Internet VoIP service could be fairly reliable, *or* it could result in poor audio quality for both VoIP lines!

The level of success varies depending on the speed of your broadband uplink, the types of applications you use on your computers, and the amount of data transmitted from and received to your home network. For example, suppose that you had a broadband link with a 256-kbps uplink speed and you have a couple of computers on your home network, each with moderate Internet activity that uses about 64 kbps of the broadband uplink. Adding a single VoIP line that consumes approximately 90 kbps of the uplink could work well and interfere infrequently with home network traffic. However, if a second VoIP line is added, now the two VoIP lines are consuming 180 kbps of the uplink, more than two-thirds of the available speed. Audio problems could definitely result when the computers on the home network send e-mail or web-browsing traffic to the Internet.

To have the best chance of success with two-line Internet VoIP service (this also applies to single-line service), consider the following recommendations:

- Talk with your high-speed broadband service provider about obtaining the highest uplink speed possible. Many services are offered at speeds of 384 kbps, 512 kbps, 1 Mbps, and even 2 Mbps. The provider might charge a premium for higher speeds, though, so you should weigh the cost/benefit ratio of the second VoIP line if you have to upgrade your broadband speed to make the service work.

- Consider reducing the bandwidth used by one or both of the VoIP lines. This might or might not be an option, depending on the service provider. For example, Vonage offers a configurable Bandwidth Saver option, where you can reduce the bandwidth used by logging on to your Vonage account website. Note that reducing the bandwidth could reduce audio quality.

- Examine the applications being used on your home network. In particular, avoid programs and services that consume significant bandwidth, such as file/music sharing, webcams, web servers, and so on.

 Many people get confused about broadband speeds. Remember that you need to consider the uplink speed, which is the most important factor for VoIP. Downlink speeds (for example, 1.5 Mbps, 2 Mbps, or 4 Mbps) are almost always several times higher than uplink speeds and typically cause few VoIP issues. Uplink speed, on the other hand, is usually a bottleneck and the source of problems if it's too slow.

If you do decide to go with a two-line VoIP service (either cable VoIP or Internet VoIP), installing the service is straightforward, as shown in Figure 11-12.

Figure 11-12 Connecting a Two-Line VoIP Service

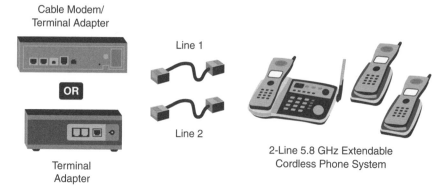

You would use two RJ11 phone cables, each plugged into the "Phone 1" and "Phone 2" ports on the terminal adapter (or integrated cable modem/terminal adapter). You could then plug each of these lines into a two-line cordless phone system.

Specialized Phone Devices

One final topic probably fits well in this chapter, which discusses wiring options, and that is a short discussion on specialized devices that also use your phone line.

Fax

Fax machines use analog phone lines (like the PSTN) to dial a remote fax machine and transmit information. Fax machines can operate over a VoIP service just like a PSTN service. Just plug the fax machine into an outlet that has VoIP access. If the fax machine and VoIP terminal adapter are collocated, use a splitter that can turn one phone jack into several (visit your friendly electronics store).

Check with your VoIP provider, though, to confirm fax support, because some providers do not currently support fax service.

TiVo and Satellite Receiver Boxes

Many home entertainment set-top boxes, such as satellite receiver dishes and TiVo boxes, use a telephone line to dial up the entertainment service and perform functions such as downloading updated software and reporting on pay-per-view movies you have watched (for billing purposes).

Some of the VoIP service providers have disclaimers on their websites indicating that these types of dialup access services might not function properly. We have not experienced any problems and we can't think of a reason why problems would occur, but we thought it prudent to pass along the disclaimer.

According to a tech note on Vonage's website, a PSTN line is required to complete the initial guided setup of TiVo, and after the initial setup, a VoIP line can be used on an ongoing basis (see http://www.vonage.com/help.php?article=389).

Again, any of these types of set-top boxes can be connected to a VoIP line through an outlet or other means, just like a phone handset.

Home Security/Alarm Systems

Many home alarm systems that are connected to a central monitoring facility use the telephone system to do so. If you have such a system, we recommend that you discuss with your security/alarm provider any potential limitations of switching from a PSTN line to a VoIP line. If you want to switch completely to VoIP service, most alarm services offer a cellular (wireless) connection option. You will incur a charge for it, but you will likely recoup the cost quickly, especially if you have high long-distance bills prior to switching.

Again, Vonage provides no support for home alarm services and recommends other (non-VoIP) options for connecting such services (see http://www.vonage.com/help.php?article=864).

Summary

We have looked at a number of options for extending VoIP throughout your home and making it easily usable. Cordless phone systems (especially two-line extendable 5.8-GHz systems) are the easiest means to extend VoIP service to everywhere you want to use it. Although it's a bit more involved, you can also use the existing telephone wiring in your home to extend VoIP service from the room where your Internet connection is located to other rooms.

The next chapter looks at a third option that might also apply to you in certain situations: using a wireless bridge to locate the terminal adapter itself in a different room than your Internet access.

CHAPTER 12

Using Wireless Networks to Extend VoIP

You have another possibility when it comes to extending VoIP service inside your home. We broke it out into a different chapter because it is a more expensive option, but it does solve a specific problem.

Wireless Bridges

Suppose that you need to have your VoIP terminal adapter in a different room of the house than your Internet access. The methods described in Chapter 11, "Making VoIP Accessible Throughout Your Home," of using either cordless phones or existing house wiring could be options. But suppose neither of those solutions was acceptable.

What if you wanted to have your Internet access (broadband modem and wireless router) in one room, say a bedroom, but you wanted a VoIP line only in a den that you use as a home office. Also, suppose that you have no existing phone jack in that room and that you want to connect a corded speakerphone that you have.

You can use an option that leverages your home wireless network, assuming that you have one. Figure 12-1 illustrates how you can do this.

Figure 12-1   Internet VoIP Setup Using a Wireless Bridge (Linksys WET54G or WGA54G)

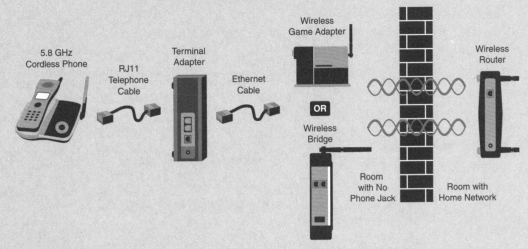

Instead of connecting the VoIP terminal adapter directly to your wireless router using an Ethernet cable, you can locate the terminal adapter in a distant room and install a wireless bridge. The wireless bridge can make the connection between the terminal adapter and the home wireless router, as a substitute for an Ethernet cable.

It's a bit out of the scope of this book, so we don't cover the installation of wireless bridges here, but a couple of products that would do the job include the Linksys WET54G Wireless Bridge and the Linksys WGA54G Wireless Game Adapter (game adapters work just like bridges).

If you need to do this and want installation help with the bridge (or game adapter), we suggest picking up a copy of our other book, *Home Networking Simplified* (by Cisco Press), which gives you step-by-step instructions. Basically you configure your bridge to link with your wireless router, just like you would with a wireless-enabled laptop.

The important thing to understand is that the terminal adapter has no knowledge that it is operating over a wireless connection to the router.

 Tip We highly recommend that you get your VoIP service working first with a wired connection between the terminal adapter and your home router before you try and insert the wireless bridge into the picture; otherwise, you might not be able to determine where the problem is if the service does not work initially.

Wireless Phone Jacks

Another option for locating your VoIP phone in a different room than the room that houses your home networking equipment is to buy a wireless phone jack. Wireless phone jacks are sold as a pair of devices that extend a phone jack to another location in your home using a wireless signal. Figure 12-2 shows the setup for this option.

Figure 12-2   Internet VoIP Setup Using a Wireless Phone Jack (RCA RC926)

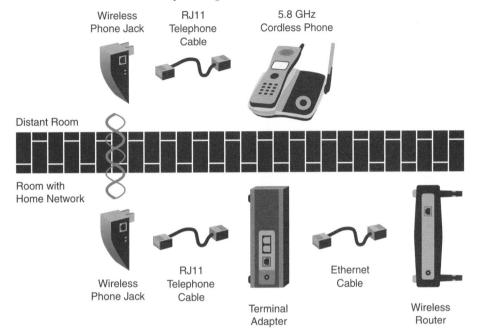

First, you would install the VoIP terminal adapter in the room next to your broadband connection and home network router, as we describe in Chapter 10, "Connecting the VoIP Equipment," and Chapter 11. Instead of plugging a handset into the terminal adapter, however, you would use an RJ11 telephone cable to connect the "Phone 1" jack on the terminal adapter to the RJ11 jack on one of the wireless phone jacks, which then gets plugged into the nearest power outlet.

Now simply take the other wireless phone jack and plug it into a wall outlet in the room where you want the VoIP phone line. Connect your phone handset to the RJ11 phone jack on the wireless phone jack using another RJ11 telephone cable.

The two wireless phone jack devices should establish a wireless connection between each other and provide a connection between the terminal adapter and the phone handset.

 People report different levels of success with wireless phone jacks. Some folks have great experiences. Others say they hear a lot of static on the connection. Remember that the wireless signal on which these devices rely is subject to interference much like other types of wireless products. So your success with these jacks will depend on the wireless signal conditions in your home.

Summary

Wireless network bridges and wireless phone jacks both provide a good solution to a unique problem. In most cases, VoIP service can be extended throughout your home with the methods discussed in Chapter 11. However, if you have unique circumstances, one of the additional options presented here can be an effective solution to the problem.

We aim to please.

CHAPTER 13

Troubleshooting: Can You Hear Me Now?

What to do if your VoIP service has issues somewhat depends on the type of service. If you have VoIP cable service, you probably need to call the cable company to repair it. It was most likely professionally installed, and if so, the cable company should ensure that it's in good working order.

If you have chosen an Internet VoIP service, you probably did a self-installation, and you probably shoulder a bit more of the burden to get it working. Don't worry though, the majority of the time, this type of service works on the first try with no problems. But if you do have issues, the rest of this chapter is for you.

Classify the Trouble

The first step to troubleshooting is to classify the type of problem you are having. Generally, VoIP service problems can be categorized into the following three major groups:

- **Service connection problems**—Getting the service working, including having the terminal adapter communicating properly with the VoIP provider

- **Voice quality issues**—Having choppy or intermittent voice issues while talking with another person

- **Dialing-related issues**—Getting a fast-busy or reorder tone when you dial

We can't solve all the possible issues with VoIP services, given the number of providers, different broadband services, and different home networking equipment that's available, but we will give it our best shot.

Service Connection Problems

If you pick up the handset and hear no dial tone, you are probably having a problem connecting to the VoIP service itself. A number of possible issues can cause the problem. We start by looking at the indicator lights on the terminal adapter. Table 13-1 shows the LEDs for a Linksys PAP2 terminal adapter. Other terminal adapters (including Linksys integrated router/terminal adapter products) most likely have similar indicators.

Table 13-1   Linksys PAP2 Terminal Adapter LEDs

	Power LED	**Ethernet LED**	**Phone 1 LED**
Off	No power or not plugged in correctly	No connection to home network router	Not able to reach broadband service provider
Blinking	Booting or trying to reach home network	Normal	Normal; call in progress
Steady	Normal	Normal	Normal; no call in progress
Red	Wrong power supply or device failure	—	—

If the Power LED is not lit, check that the terminal adapter is plugged into an electrical outlet. Without power, the terminal adapter cannot function (and neither can your VoIP service). If the Power LED is blinking, the terminal adapter is in the process of booting up; give it a few seconds. Depending on the model of terminal adapter you use, you can have different types of LEDs blinking with their own meanings; check your terminal adapter documentation for more details. Figure 13-1 shows normal operation for a Linksys PAP2 terminal adapter.

Figure 13-1   Normal Terminal Adapter Operation, Indicated by LEDs

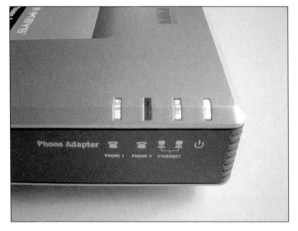

If the Ethernet LED is lit (refer to Figure 13-1 again), the terminal adapter has made a connection to your home router. If it's not lit, a problem exists between your router and the terminal adapter. Check the Ethernet cable to make sure that it's connected properly. Try a different Ethernet cable to see whether the one you are using is faulty. Also, double-check that your home router is providing dynamic IP addresses, which the terminal adapter needs to get connected to your home network. You can do this by accessing your home router and verifying that DHCP is enabled. See your router's documentation for the procedure to locate this information.

Note If you intentionally set up your home network to use static IP addressing, see Chapter 10, "Connecting the VoIP Equipment," for manually configuring the terminal adapter to use a static IP address. If you don't understand what we are talking about, your home network is most likely using dynamic IP addressing, and this is not an issue. Some terminal adapters have a way to check through a handset whether the device is getting an IP address. For example, with the Linksys PAP2, you can dial **110#** and the terminal adapter will give you an audio message with its assigned IP address.

Finally, check whether the Phone1 LED is lit (see Figure 13-1). If it is not lit, a problem exists in reaching the VoIP provider over your Internet connection. Check whether you can reach the Internet from a computer on your home network. If not, your Internet service could be causing the problem.

If the terminal adapter seems to be functioning normally and the indicator lights are showing normal, try these other remedies:

- Check the handset you are using to make sure that it works properly. Try plugging it into a public switched telephone network (PSTN) phone jack, or try a different handset.

- If you are using cordless handsets, try using a corded handset to make sure that the problem is not with your cordless phone handset.

- Lift the handset off hook while it is plugged into the terminal adapter and listen to the earpiece. Some terminal adapters can play audio diagnostic messages. For example, the Linksys PAP2 can tell you whether you inadvertently plugged the phone into the "Phone 2" instead of the "Phone 1" jack.

- Recheck the cabling between the terminal adapter and the handset to make sure that it is connected properly.

- Try a different RJ11 phone cable to see whether the one you are using is faulty.

- Try resetting the power on the terminal adapter (unplug it and plug it back in).

- Try rebooting your home network router.

- Try rebooting your broadband modem.

- Take the terminal adapter and handset to a friend's or family member's house that has broadband service and try it there.

If you need to reset your broadband connection, it's best to power down both the broadband modem and your home network router and wait for a minute or two. Then, power on the broadband modem first, wait a minute, power on the home router, wait a minute, and then power on computers and other devices connected to your home network.

If you have tried all these remedies without success, it's time to call your VoIP provider. You could have a problem with the subscription itself. Perhaps an incorrect MAC address was typed in for the terminal adapter, or perhaps the service was not activated properly.

 When all hope seems lost, try what we like to call the "ten-minute miracle." Power everything down and go do something else for ten minutes. This might reset the equipment and can also help clear your head.

Voice Quality Issues

Voice quality issues with VoIP services are possible, just like any other form of voice communication. To start with, it helps to define what type of voice quality issue you are dealing with (this also presumes that you have dial tone and can make and receive calls).

If you hear static on the call, the problem is probably not with the VoIP service. Because VoIP relies on digital packets to send and receive information, voice quality issues tend to be noticed as "choppy" voice or intermittent speech, missing parts of words. Static can be caused by the phone line of the person you are talking to or the handset you are using. If you are using a cordless phone, try standing closer to the base unit and change the channel that your phone is using (a button to swap channels on the phone is usually visible).

 Before assuming that a voice quality problem is the result of the service itself, always make sure that you have tried connecting a known-to-be-working, corded phone handset directly to the terminal adapter. Many voice quality issues perceived to be a service problem turn out to be caused by the person's cordless telephone. Nothing is more embarrassing than yelling at the VoIP provider's customer service tech for an hour, only to learn that your cordless phone is cutting out every time your kids make microwave popcorn.

The "choppy" voice problem can be caused by several issues, including the speed of your broadband connection, the quality of the broadband provider's network, or some other issue. These items are discussed in the next few sections.

Broadband Speed

VoIP services consume part of the speed of your broadband connection to send and receive the packets that carry your voice conversation. Therefore, it's important that your broadband service speed be sufficient to carry the VoIP conversation and to provide the bandwidth needed by computers on your home network, for applications such as e-mail and instant messaging (IM).

Cable VoIP services typically use dedicated bandwidth that is set aside only for the VoIP packets, so speed of the broadband connection is not as important. If you have cable VoIP service, you can skip most of this section.

For Internet VoIP services, speed varies by VoIP provider, but most widely deployed services require 90 kbps for a voice conversation.

One simple test you can do is to see how much speed your broadband connection is providing. Using a computer on your home network, use one of the following websites to test your broadband speed (uplink speed is most important):

http://www.broadbandreports.com/stest

http://pcpitstop.com/internet/

The results should be close to what your broadband (click **Measure Upload Speed**) provider sold you. About the minimum you can use is 128 kbps, but we recommend at least 256 or 384 kbps for problem-free service. Figure 13-2 shows an example test using Broadbandreports.com. Keep in mind that this test is not always accurate, so don't fret about not achieving exactly 256 or 384 kbps, but your speed should be close to your provider's claims (assuming that nothing else is running on your home network). In this case, the uplink speed was measured at 351 kbps, more than enough for VoIP service and most other computer applications running on our home network.

Figure 13-2   Testing Your Broadband Speed

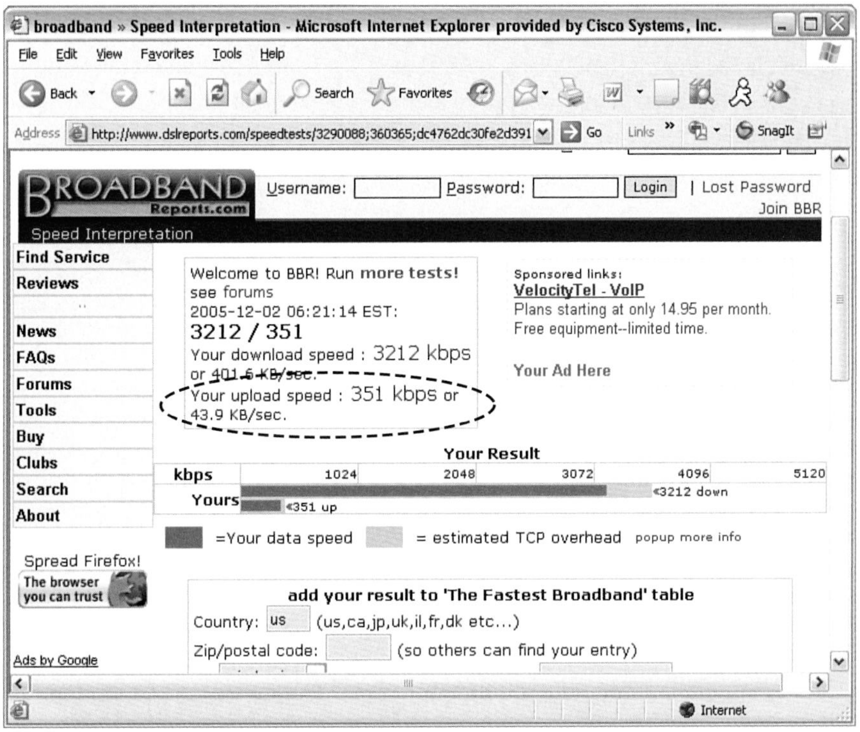

If you seem to have enough bandwidth, you can also try disconnecting the computers from your home network and making another call. If the issue goes away, your broadband speed might not be sufficient for both the VoIP service and the computer applications you are using. Check to see whether you can upgrade to a higher broadband speed.

Alternatively, you might want to check the computers on your home network to see whether applications are consuming excessive bandwidth on your broadband connection. Computer viruses are one possibility. Other bandwidth consumers are file- and music-sharing programs, such as Lime Wire and BitTorrent, which are popular with teenagers (and adults). Aside from the debate over their legality, these programs can consume lots of your broadband speed. Downloading is not much of an issue, but if you are uploading a lot of files (that is, others are downloading from you), that can be a problem.

 You can also check your computer for spyware, which can consume a lot of bandwidth. If you have never checked your computer for spyware, you probably have some running on it.

Another possible remedy is to try reducing the amount of bandwidth required for a VoIP call. This can impact voice quality slightly but not nearly as much as not having enough bandwidth. Vonage provides an option to reduce the VoIP bandwidth from the default of 90 kbps (High) to 50 kbps (Medium) or 30 kbps (Low). Try the medium setting and see whether it helps.

If you find that the speed of a broadband cable connection is lacking, make sure that you have not "split" the cable too many times before it gets to your modem. For example, if the cable coming into your house splits off to three rooms and in one of those rooms you split the cable between your TV and your modem, the modem is getting only one-sixth of the signal strength coming into your house. Try running a cable (without splitting) to your modem. If the problem doesn't go away, you can have a cable technician run a "dedicated line" to your modem or you can buy a cable signal amplifier (the price for either won't be much different).

Broadband Network Quality

Assuming that you have enough broadband speed and that's not the issue, you could also have a problem in the broadband provider's network itself.

Generally the Internet is overbuilt (meaning that it has more than enough capacity) and offers extremely high-speed connections, but we have seen at least one broadband provider that has built a … how shall we put this … sucky network. You get great speed from your house to its network, and then your packets take forever to make it across the provider's network and to the Internet.

So to rule this out, you can again do a quick test to see how fast your packets are getting to the Internet. Using a computer on your home network go to this website:

http://pcpitstop.com/internet/

Click **Measure Ping Times**. The results are displayed as a table of green, yellow, or red bars on the screen. For good voice quality, you should see all green bars (meaning less than 200 milliseconds of delay). If you see yellow or red, this could be contributing to your voice quality issue. Talk to your broadband provider. The techies refer to this issue as *latency,* which is nothing more than delay, and *jitter,* which is the variability of the delay. Both of these issues, if bad enough, can cause quality issues.

Figure 13-3 shows some sample results of this test. In this case, the delay of 49–112 milliseconds listed in the Average column is well within the recommended limits for VoIP delay. Again, this test is not highly accurate and can vary each time you run it, but it can give you an idea of your provider's quality.

Figure 13-3   Determining How Fast Your Sent Packets Make It to the Internet

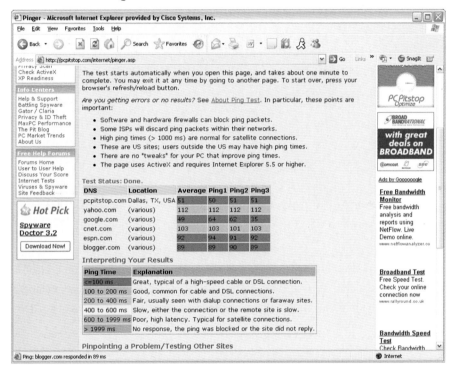

Similarly, the broadband network might be fast enough but might be losing too many packets (it's rare, but it can happen). Again, a simple test can show you whether this is an issue. Using a computer on your home network go to the following website and click **Trace Routes**:

http://pcpitstop.com/internet/

The results are displayed in a table. Look at the column labeled Loss % in Figure 13-4. For good voice quality, you should see little or nothing in this column. More than about 1–5 percent could be contributing to your voice quality issue.

Figure 13-4   Testing for Packet Loss to Ensure Good Voice Quality

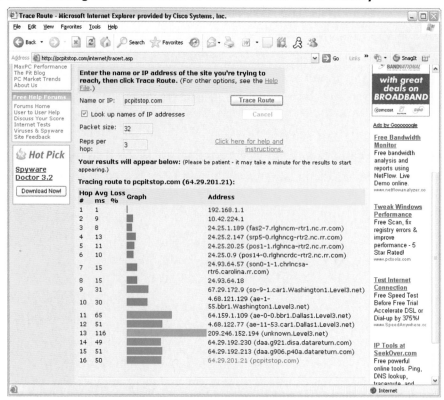

The results in Figure 13-4 show no loss, so this is excellent for VoIP service. If you see packet loss from this test, it could be a definite issue, and you should talk to your broadband provider. You might have an intermittent problem with your broadband connection itself or with the local portion (the last mile) of the provider's network.

Note You can select which web server you run the test on (the default is Pcpitstop.com). Some servers disable responses to the packets used for this test for security reasons, so they can show up as complete packet loss. If you modify the web server and the test fails, rerun the test to Pcpitstop.com before assuming you have a problem.

Sometimes people add splitters to the cable connection inside their home. The splitters are convenient, but they can cause issues with your home network and broadband cable Internet access. If you are having intermittent issues with your cable connection, make sure that you have not added a splitter between the cable junction box and your cable modem.

Another common issue with intermittent broadband problems is forgetting to put a digital subscriber line (DSL) filter on all your phone jacks except the jack with the DSL modem.

Other Issues

Other possible issues that can cause poor voice quality include the following:

- A 2.4-GHz cordless phone (or even a microwave oven) and your wireless network could be interfering with each other. Try a corded handset and see whether the issue goes away. If so, consider replacing your 2.4-GHz cordless phone with a 5.8-GHz cordless phone.

- Periodically, power glitches might put your broadband modem, home network router, or VoIP terminal adapter in a "stuck" state. Try powering them all off and restarting them in the following order, waiting a minute or so between each one: broadband modem, home router, and VoIP terminal adapter.

Dialing-Related Issues

The most common issues related to dialing are receiving a fast-busy or reorder tone when you dial a number. Consider the following remedies:

- Are you dialing a number in a different area code than your VoIP number? If so, make sure that you use 10-digit dialing.

- Some area codes, such as 900 and 976, are blocked from dialing on VoIP services.

- Sometimes providers of toll-free 800 numbers specify a "zone" within which they accept calls. If you have an area code on your VoIP service number outside that zone, the 800 number owner might be blocking that area code, thinking that you are far away, even if you are just across the street.

Getting Additional Help from Your VoIP Provider

If all else fails, either call the help line of your VoIP provider and/or check out its website for additional troubleshooting help.

The following are useful websites:

http://www.vonage.com/help.php

https://www.callvantage.att.com/help/index.htm

Summary

VoIP services are easy to install and use, but they rely on the stability of your home network and on the adequacy and reliability of your broadband Internet service. The troubleshooting steps covered in this chapter can get you through the majority of issues that arise. If these steps fail, contact your VoIP provider for additional assistance.

Of course, it's always a good option to place a call to the Geek Squad folks. They are familiar with both home networks and VoIP services and are sure to be a great source of help.

CHAPTER 14

From the Geek Squad Files

When you set up a Voice over IP (VoIP) service, remember that your phone is now part of your home network. If your network is just average, that is, if you lose your Internet connection a lot or you have really slow downloads, you will probably not get the best performance out of the Internet telephone service either. Consider the following items:

- **Planning**—Do some planning up-front to save yourself headaches later. Think about how you and your family use the phone(s) in your house today. How will they use them after you install VoIP service? Have a plan for how you will connect the phone service(s) (including public switched telephone network and VoIP, single or multiple lines, and so on) to the phone handsets in your home. Will you use all your existing handsets or purchase newer handsets? Are your handsets wired or cordless? It might help to make a diagram of your house and map out where you have, need, or want phones.

- **Installation**—If your VoIP provider (especially if it's the cable company) installs the service, be sure to specify whether you want the company to replace your existing phone lines. Some overly enthusiastic installers might start cutting the wiring at your junction box before they do the inside installation.

- **Alarm systems**—Some home alarm systems are not compatible with Internet telephony. If you have one of these alarm systems, check with the company that monitors the system. Many of these companies offer a cellular option. If you are saving a lot of money by switching to VoIP, it might be worth the cost to get the cellular option for the alarm system (if required).

- **Extending with wireless**—Remember that some cordless phones can interfere with a wireless network signal. Check the frequency of your wireless home network gear. Be sure that the frequency your phone uses (it's usually written on the phone) and the frequency your wireless network equipment uses (it's usually written on the equipment or the box) are different. For example, if you are using an 802.11g wireless home network, it operates at 2.4 GHz, so you should buy 5.8 GHz cordless phones to avoid interference.

- **Power**—In case you have not heard this before, if you lose power, you will lose your Internet telephony service unless you have backup power (even then, you may still lose your service). All kidding aside, you should consider getting an uninterruptible power supply (UPS). This can give you a couple of hours of battery power for your modem and your cordless phones if you lose power to your house. Then again, consider your cell phone as a backup.

PART IV

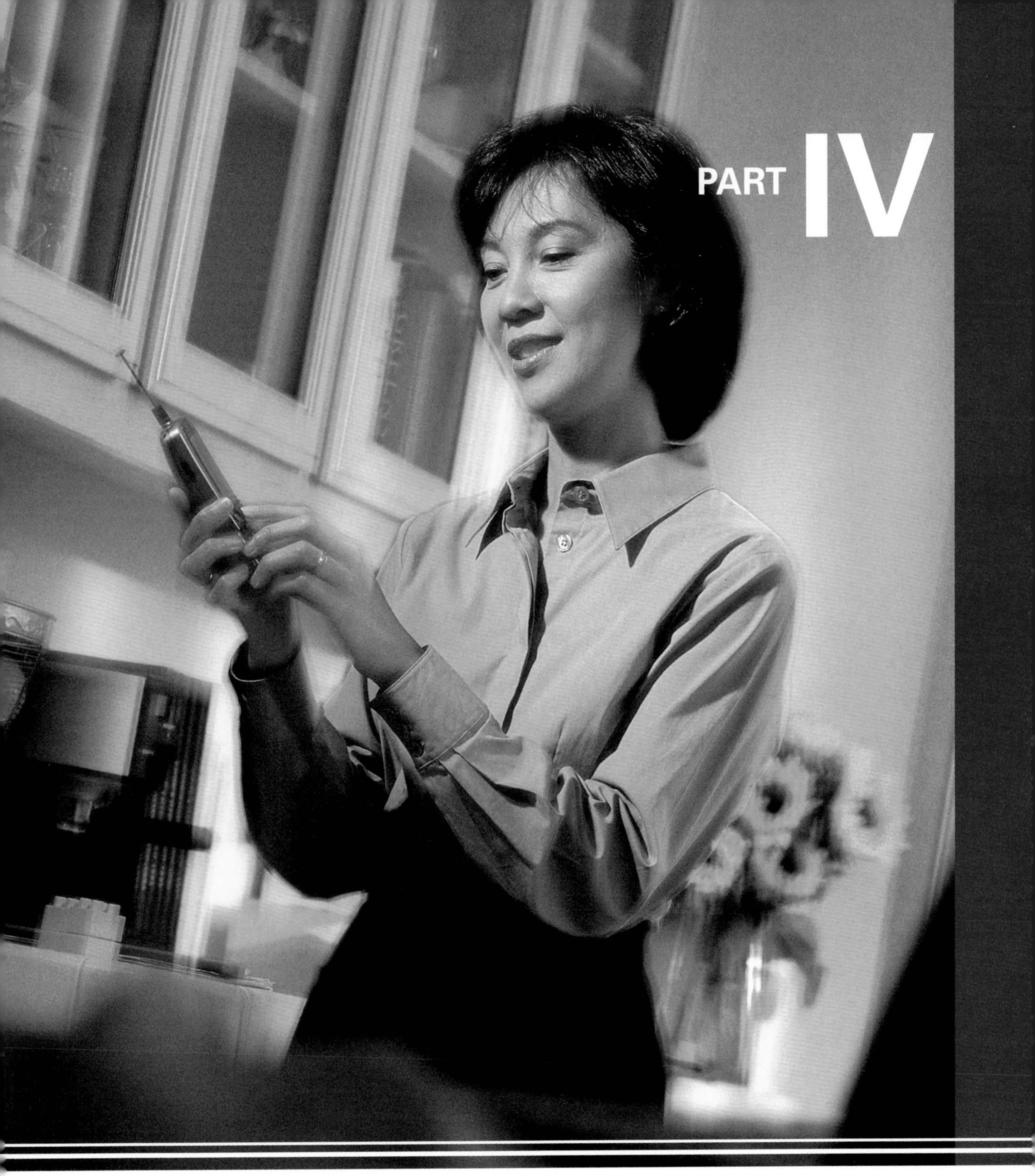

PART IV

VoIP Chat Services

The last part of the book explores the latest way to use VoIP service: over an instant message–type client. Referred to as *VoIP chat,* this type of service is discussed in Chapter 15, "VoIP Chat Services." VoIP chat works much differently than the other types of VoIP, and we explain these important differences here.

If you are interested in using VoIP chat (which is free between people who use the same program), we explain how to choose a client and how to get started in Chapter 16, "Using Skype and Google Talk." One of these services also allows you to make and receive calls to or from PSTN (for a low fee), and we show you how to get this set up, too.

We end the book with a chapter on the future of telephony. A lot of changes in voice technology have occurred over the last several years, and the pace does not appear to be slowing. We walk you through a possible future scenario to give you an idea of where folks in the industry think this is all going.

CHAPTER 15

VoIP Chat Services

This chapter takes a look at VoIP chat services, which provide the same basic function as Internet telephony but are different in the way they operate.

In Chapter 1, "Traditional Phone Systems," we spent some time discussing the public switched telephone network (PSTN) as the foundation or starting parting point of VoIP. In this chapter, we discuss the foundation of VoIP chat services, which has nothing to do with telephony; rather, it's instant messaging (IM). Bet you didn't see that coming!

Instant Messaging

For those of you who don't have the "bug" yet, instant messaging is a chat service that allows you to create a two-person (or multiperson) "chat room" for real-time communication. Most of the standard instant messaging services allow you to identify common contacts or buddies who you can communicate with. When someone on your "buddy list" is online, you are both notified of each other's availability. Double-clicking the person's name opens a window where the two of you can communicate through typed messages. This technology is amazingly convenient, very useful, highly addictive, and at times, extremely annoying.

Note *Real time* means that you experience no delay between the time you send information and the time it is received. E-mail usually involves a delay. You send a message and the recipient reads it sometime later. Real-time communications like IM happen instantaneously. You type a message on your computer, and it appears on the recipient's screen at nearly the same time.

Here's how IM works:

Instant messaging services require you to download a program, or client, to your computer. This program connects to a messaging service that allows parties to communicate. At first blush, it might sound a lot like e-mail or Internet telephony, but some key differences exist.

The first big difference is that unlike e-mail, where it doesn't matter whether the person you are communicating with is online, or Internet telephony, where you have to dial someone's phone number to see whether she is available, with IM, you maintain a list of people who you want to chat with. When you have your IM client open (that is, when you activate the program), you are connected to a database. At that point, you can see which of your "buddies" are online, and all your buddies who are also online are notified of your status. You can add others to your list or be added to other people's list. Sometimes the other person is notified through e-mail and has to approve your request to add him to your contact list.

The other main difference between IM and other tools such as e-mail and Internet telephony is that IM is a *peer-to-peer* system as opposed to the *client-server* model used my most other communication systems. The sections that follow provide a summary of each type of system.

Client-Server

In a client-server system, most of the intelligence in the system is located in a central server (or distributed among a few central servers). The clients in these systems have minimal capabilities and are almost always a drain on the system, adding to the computing burden of the servers. In a well-designed system, enough capacity exists to handle many clients, but you always have the possibility that excessive client usage can overwhelm the system.

 One of the first "live" Internet events was a Victoria's Secret fashion show (in February 1999). Apparently someone (probably an IT person) underestimated how many people (read men, ages 12–102) would be interested in seeing gorgeous women walking around in their underwear. Needless to say, the servers had a massive overload crash about 3 minutes into the event.

The PSTN can largely be viewed as a client-server system, with the central offices being the servers and the phone handsets being the clients. Cable TV and satellite TV are other examples of client-server systems, with the cable or satellite system being the server and the cable/satellite set-top box in your home being the client. Most websites are client-server systems as well, with the website being the server and your Internet browser being the client. The following figure shows a map of a client-server network.

Peer-to-Peer

In a peer-to-peer system, resources are shared among all the clients using the system at any given time. As in the client-server model, each client that joins the system puts a burden on the system, but unlike client-server models, each client also provides computing resources to the system. Therefore, as more people join the network, the network becomes more powerful. Some peer-to-peer networks do rely on limited servers, typically for directory services. Directory services help users in a peer-to-peer network find other users.

Others (called *true peer-to-peer networks*) have no servers and rely completely on the individual clients. Walkie-talkies are probably the simplest example of a peer-to-peer system. No central system is required for them to operate; they communicate directly with each other.

Client-Server Model

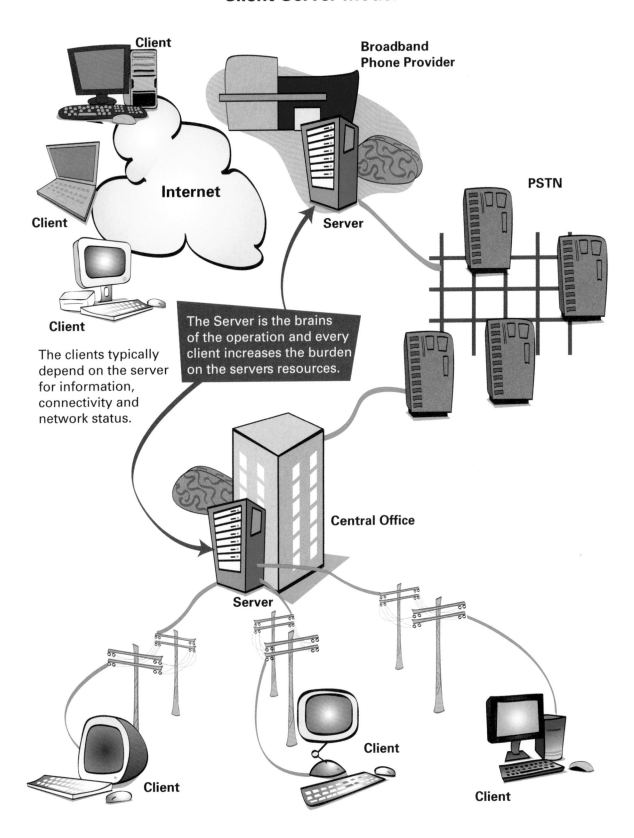

Client

Broadband Phone Provider

Internet

PSTN

Client

Client

Server

The Server is the brains of the operation and every client increases the burden on the servers resources.

The clients typically depend on the server for information, connectivity and network status.

Central Office

Server

Client

Client

Client

Peer-to-Peer Networks

In some peer-to-peer networks (such as IM), there's a directory server which allows users to log in and "find" each other.

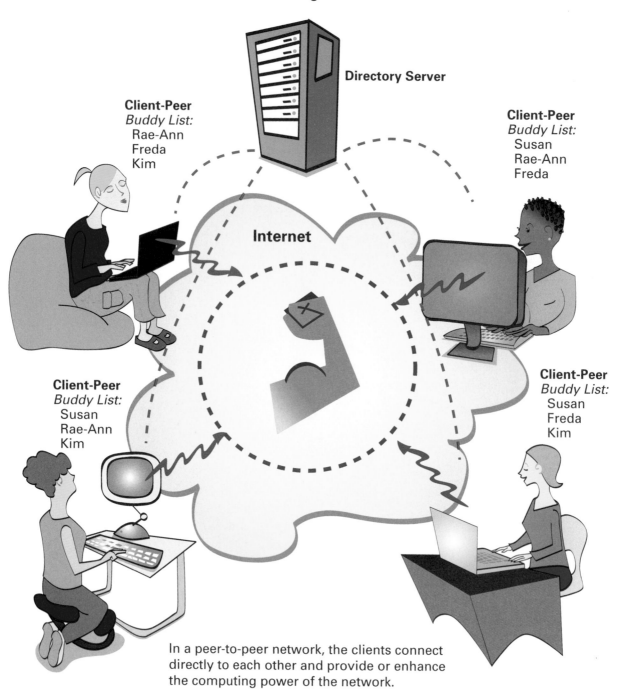

Directory Server

Client-Peer
Buddy List:
Rae-Ann
Freda
Kim

Client-Peer
Buddy List:
Susan
Rae-Ann
Freda

Internet

Client-Peer
Buddy List:
Susan
Rae-Ann
Kim

Client-Peer
Buddy List:
Susan
Freda
Kim

In a peer-to-peer network, the clients connect directly to each other and provide or enhance the computing power of the network.

The following figure shows a map of a peer-to-peer network.

What matters in all of this is that when you use one of these IM clients, you have a list of folks you like to chat with, you can see when they are online and available to communicate with, and you have no complicated setup; you just click a person's name and type away.

Note One downside of IM is that most IM clients (the big ones being Yahoo! Messenger, AOL Instant Messenger, and MSN Messenger) use proprietary languages so that you can't chat with a buddy if you use AIM and she uses MSN Messenger. A workaround to this is to install a "translator" program such as Trillian, Everybuddy, or Proteus. These programs allow you to communicate with multiple IM protocols in a single client. You still need to create an account with each service (most of which are free), but you can use all of them through a single client (program) running on your machine.

Trillian is also the name of the main female character in *The Hitchhiker's Guide to the Galaxy,* one of the all-time great sci-fi books that doesn't involve Spock.

Internet Messaging with Voice

At this point, you are probably wondering what all of this has to do with VoIP. Well, soon after IM became popular, two clever guys who had already created one of the biggest peer-to-peer file-sharing systems figured out that after an IM conversation was established, you had two computers sharing packets. Because a packet is a packet is a packet, why not just make them voice packets and avoid all that annoying typing. Easy, right?

Well, it was pretty easy. Most computers today have a great deal of computing capacity, more than enough to convert your analog voice waves to a digital stream and then stuff all those 1s and 0s into packets, see Chapter 2, "Voice over IP (VoIP)". In addition, most computers have built-in speakers and microphones and high-speed access to the Internet. So let's see:

- Microphone, check.

- Speaker, check.

- Processor to perform digital conversion, check.

- Lots of bandwidth, check.

- Connection to someone else with the same stuff, check.

- Yep, we can have a conversation!

Some limitations exist regarding the sound quality (as always, the quality of the conversation itself is up to you). Just as with standard VoIP, bandwidth and delay can greatly affect sound quality. Unlike VoIP, however, VoIP chat does not require dedicated hardware such as a terminal adapter or even a phone. If you are using the microphone and speakers on your PC and they are not of the highest quality (our publisher frowned on the term *crappy*), the sound will suffer. Finally, if you are running a lot of programs on your PC or even a single program that is processor intensive, the sound quality for you and the person on the other end can suffer.

You can buy some cool gadgets such as headsets. We discuss some of the options in the next chapter as well as some guidelines for when they make sense.

Unlike either the PSTN or Internet VoIP services, VoIP chat services are typically not "always on," meaning people can reach you only when your computer is turned on, the VoIP chat program is running, and you are logged into the directory server for the VoIP chat service. Otherwise, you are unreachable.

Another limitation with these services is that while they are free, they are also proprietary, so you can only talk with other folks who use the same service. (At this time, no "Trillian" equivalent to "VoIP" chat services is available.)

On the other hand, at least one of the major VoIP chat services provides a fee-based service that enables you to dial a standard PSTN number from your VoIP chat client and also allows you to purchase a virtual phone number so that people can call your VoIP chat client from a standard phone (PTSN, cellular, or VoIP). Really cool stuff. The following figure shows how VoIP chat services can communicate with phones on the PSTN.

By the way, the two guys that we mentioned who came up with this are Niklas Zennström and Janus Friis, creators of both Kazaa and Skype. (Skype is one of the VoIP chat systems we discuss in the next chapter.) In 2005, eBay purchased Skype for a gazillion dollars (it was actually $2.6 billion in cash and stock, with an additional $1.5 billion in incentives), making Niklas and Janus very wealthy men. Good for them! Creating one great program could be a fluke, but two great programs leaves no doubt as to their talents, and in our opinion, really smart people should be rich.

How VoIP Chat Works with Other Systems

The ability to dial into a VoIP chat from the PSTN (VoIP)
is only available with Skype (as a beta) at the time of this writing.
With this service you pay to have a phone number. When someone
calls the number it rings your VoIP chat client.

To dial out to a PSTN (or VoIP) phone requires an
additional program (Skype's version is called SkypeOut).
With this program you pay into an account and you
are charged on a per minute usage rate which is quite affordable.

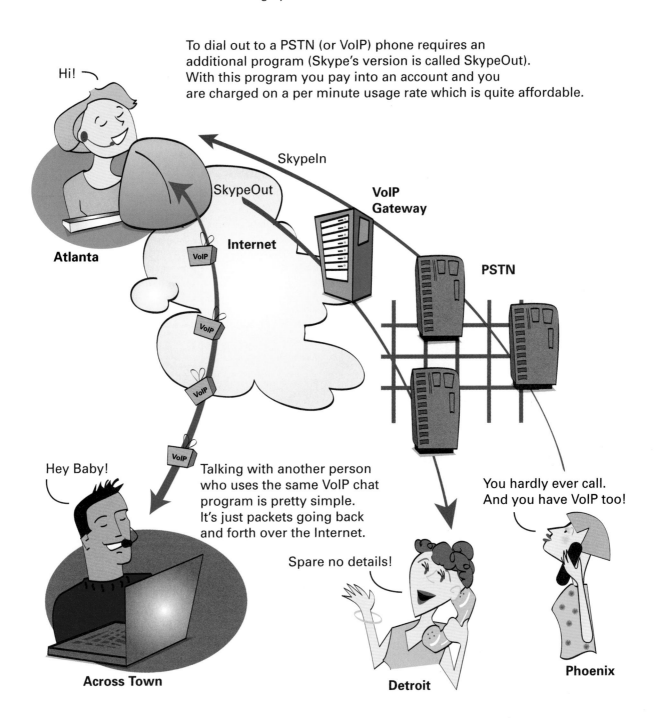

Hi!

Atlanta

SkypeIn

SkypeOut

VoIP
Gateway

Internet

VoIP

VoIP

VoIP

VoIP

PSTN

Hey Baby!

Talking with another person
who uses the same VoIP chat
program is pretty simple.
It's just packets going back
and forth over the Internet.

Spare no details!

You hardly ever call.
And you have VoIP too!

Across Town

Detroit

Phoenix

Summary

The next chapter looks at how to install and use two of the most common VoIP chat services, Skype and Google Talk.

Now that we have introduced VoIP chat services, it's worthwhile to compare it to the previously discussed type of phone services (PSTN and Internet VoIP). Table 15-1 summarizes the features for PSTN, VoIP, and VoIP chat services.

Table 15-1   Comparison of PSTN, VoIP, and VoIP Chat Features

	PSTN	VoIP	VoIP Chat
Network Model	Client–server.	Client-server.	Peer-to-peer.
911	Enhanced 911 (E911) in most places; 911 in others.	Ranges from E911 to 911 to nothing. Always know what your provider's policy is.	Nope, not even close.
Power	Provided by the telephone network.	Runs off your house power.	Runs off your PC power and what powers your Internet connection.
Off-Net Calling	If someone has a number, you can call it . . . but your rate probably stinks.	Reaches virtually any phone number, and the rate is dirt cheap . . . maybe even free.	It's all free on the peer-to-peer network. If you want to send to or receive calls from the PSTN or VoIP, you have to pay (assuming that your provider offers this service).
Quality	As good as it gets.	Ranges from really good to cell phone quality, but it's mostly good and can be made very good for extra money.	Depends on your PC and your audio equipment. With the minimum required equipment, the quality is not great.
Reliability	Usually always on.	Based on the reliability of your Internet connection, which is probably very good.	Based on the reliability of your Internet connection, which is probably very good.

CHAPTER 16

Using Skype and Google Talk

In this chapter, we look at two of the VoIP chat services (Skype and Google Talk) in greater detail. We're not going into an exhaustive account of how to install these programs because they're pretty easy to install. However, we cover some tips that can help you during installation and initial use. We also look at some of the cooler features of each service.

Note Several other good VoIP chat programs, such as Gizmo Project and Yahoo! Messenger with Voice, are available. Gizmo Project has a similar feature set to Skype, and Yahoo! Messenger with Voice is similar to Google Talk. They all work similarly, so we picked two to discuss in depth.

Installing and Using Skype

Installing Skype is easy. Go to http://www.skype.com and click the **Download** link at the top of the page. As Figure 16-1 shows, Skype works with all the major operating systems. Follow the instructions for downloading the file.

Figure 16-1   Downloading Skype for Your Operating System

When the program is finished downloading to your computer, a setup wizard walks you through installation. The program asks you to create a username and password. If the username is taken, you are offered alternate suggestions. The program also asks for your full name, your country of origin, and your e-mail address.

Note You are not required to enter any information into your Skype personal profile, including your name or e-mail address, but we suggest that you enter at least an e-mail address. Skype uses your e-mail address to help other Skype users find you, and Skype promises to keep your address private.

After you have chosen a unique username, the Skype Client appears and launches a Getting Started wizard, as shown in Figure 16-2. The wizard first checks your sound settings. Simply click the **Skype Test Call** button in the Skype window. You should hear a recording welcoming you to Skype, which asks you to record a message (say anything you want; Skype trashes it afterward). The wizard then plays the message back to you. If you can hear your own voice, you are good to go. If you don't hear your voice or if you don't hear the recording, make sure that your speakers are not muted.

Figure 16-2   Skype Getting Started Wizard

Note Skype has a good online troubleshooting tool, so there's no point in duplicating it here. If you have a relatively new PC or laptop, you most likely have a built-in microphone and speaker, so any problem is usually related to an audio setting. Click the **Help** button at http://www.skype.com, and you will most likely find the solution.

After you pass the audio test, you are ready to talk to someone, but first you need someone to talk to. This is accomplished by creating a contacts list. You can do this in one of the following ways:

■ Click the **Add Contact** button and search for a specific person by typing in the full name, e-mail address, or Skype username.

 Note For fun, type in your last name, and a list of other Skype users with the same last name spools out. Double-click one name from some far-away place, and see whether that person wants to chat. (You can type a message in the Add Contact window letting the person know who you are and why you want to connect to her.) Don't worry if she is halfway around the world; it's free! Use this option with a bit of care, though. People are sensitive to spam. Being polite helps.

■ Click the **Tools** tab and choose **Import Contacts**. This opens another wizard that searches the contacts or address books of any e-mail programs you have running. It then searches the Skype user database for "hits" on the e-mail addresses in your address books. If the wizard finds any, you have the option of adding that person as a contact. This is a slick feature to get your contact list started quickly. You can also send e-mail to contacts that the wizard didn't find and ask them to join Skype.

Either way, anyone you add to your contact list needs to approve your request before you can call him, and you must approve any request for others to add you to their contacts list. This is a good way to keep people from making a nuisance of themselves. Also keep in mind that folks who have approved to have you in their contact list can see whether you are online, which is similar to instant messaging (IM) programs.

That's all there is to it if you want to talk only to other Skype users and you are happy with the audio quality. If you want to add some extra features or enhance the audio quality, read on.

Improving Your Audio Quality

The first thing to consider with regard to audio quality is the amount of packets you are stuffing into your Internet pipe. In most cases, you need to worry only about the amount of stuff you are sending and not as much about the stuff you are receiving, because most residential broadband connections provide much more downlink speed than uplink speed. Nothing kills your audio quality like a big e-mail attachment that you send, so if you really need to hear and be heard, think before clicking that **Send** button. See the tips in Chapter 13, "Troubleshooting: Can You Hear Me Now," for more on this.

 In addition to e-mails, programs that require a lot of computing power (such as active virus scans) can degrade your audio quality. VoIP chat programs use a lot of computer power.

While you can get away with using the microphone and speaker that came with your computer, the sound quality for both you and the person you are talking to will be lacking in most cases. Because you have no earpiece, your conversations will not be private. A number of accessories are available, ranging from a simple earbud and mic (much like a hands-free setup for your cell phone) all the way to a dual-mode cordless phone that works with your regular phone and your Skype account at the same time (this is so cool we can hardly stand it).

Follow these recommendations:

- **Simple earpiece and mic available as a starter kit**—With this setup, you also get some SkypeOut credit. We suggest that you start here and see how it works. You might find that this works fine, in which case you don't have to spend much money.

  Skype Pack was the only earbud-and-mic package offered on the Skype product page when this book was written.

> **Note** If you choose an earpiece-type mic, make sure that it is compatible with the audio jacks on your PC. Your hands-free cell phone setup will probably not work with your PC.

- **Headsets**—A number of headsets of varying quality are available, including a wireless Bluetooth headset. If you are a heavy user or avid online gamer, this is the way to go. Headsets are also good if you need to type and talk at the same time.

  Here are two headsets that we recommend:

  — The Logitech Internet Chat Headset is a good entry-level headset.

  — A couple of steps up is the Logitech Premium USB Headset 350.

  Both of these products are offered through the Skype product page.

  Another good place to look for headsets is http://www.plantronics.com. Most of the Plantronics headsets (and a bunch of them are available) can be ordered with USB adapters, making them ideal for VoIP chat. You can also use them with most phones too.

- **Phone handsets**—A number of corded phones are available for Skype users. Most of these phones tie in directly with your Skype account, allowing you to see your contacts list and dial out to regular numbers. A few cordless phones are also available for those who do not want to be tied to their PC (including the one that simultaneously works with your landline). Keep in mind that the range on these phones is about the same as that of regular cordless phones, but the sound quality can decrease dramatically when you get near the maximum range.

  At the high end of the spectrum is the DualPhone 3055, which works with both your VoIP chat and a standard phone line (VoIP or public switched telephone network [PSTN]) at the same time. You can also launch calls to your online Skype contacts with this. Very cool.

> When using dual-mode phones, make sure that you know which system you are using or that call to Singapore might end up costing a lot more than you thought it would!

The Linksys CIT200 cordless phone has a small base that plugs into your USB port and has a standard cordless phone so that you can walk and talk. Keep in mind that these cordless phones present additional opportunities for poor quality or interference, so unless you really need to pace while you talk, you might want to try it before you buy it.

At the lower end of the price range are corded USB phones. The ECCB Simply Phone is reasonably priced and available through the Skype page. These phones have cords, so you are tethered to your PC while talking. (The pictures of the phones do their best to not show the cord, which we find odd.)

Table 16-1 outlines the chat gear and our recommendations.

Table 16-1   VoIP Chat Gear Recommendations

Category	Notes	Relative Price	Our Recommendations
Earbud and mic	This earpiece with integrated microphone comes with Skype Pack, which gives you some SkypeOut credit.	$	This is a great piece of gear to start with. It might be all you need.
Headsets	Headsets leave your hands free while talking. They usually connect to your USB port. The Logitech Internet Chat Headset is a good entry-level headset. A couple of steps up is the Logitech Premium USB Headset 350. Many price options are available in this category.	$$–$$$	In our opinion, headsets are the best option for using voice chat programs. The quality is good, and you have your hands free to type.
Phone handsets	You can purchase hand-held phones that tie in directly with your Skype account, allowing you to see your contacts list and dial out to regular numbers.	$–$$	This option does not make much sense to us. The corded phones require you to use your hands and you are tied to the computer. The cordless versions do not offer good range.
Dual-mode phones	The DUALPhone 3055 and others like it work with both your VoIP chat and a standard phone line (VoIP or PSTN) at the same time.	$$$$	This is a high-end option recommended for power users only.

Calling People Who Have "Real" Phones (and Phone Numbers)

By now you have probably noticed the tab on the Skype client labeled **Dial** (see Figure 16-3). At the bottom of this screen is a note advising that you can call landlines (PSTN or VoIP) or mobile phones with the purchase of Skype credit. This feature is called SkypeOut, referring to outbound calls from Skype service to the PSTN.

Figure 16-3   Calling a Landline with Skype

Clicking the **purchase Skype Credit** link brings you to a sign-in screen on the Skype web page (use the same password as you do on your Skype client) and then to a screen where you can purchase SkypeOut credit. This credit allows you to call any phone number in the world (local, national, or international) at a reasonable rate. The credit is purchased in $11–$13 increments. (The base currency was in euros at the time of publication. This is likely to change because Skype was purchased by U.S.-based eBay.) This amount can give you from 8 to 11 hours of talk time, depending on where you call from and to.

After you pay for credits, you can use the dial keypad to call your friends on their cell phones or landlines in Mongolia or New York for next to nothing. Skype can also store the numbers that you dial in your contacts lists. The tally of your remaining credits is listed on the dial screen so that you know when you need to buy more.

Getting Calls from People Who Use "Real" Phones

Another great feature of Skype is the ability to receive incoming calls from landlines or mobile phones (and lest we forget, VoIP phones) directly to your Skype client by downloading the SkypeIn program add-on. This feature (in beta status at the time of publication) is available in several countries, including the United States, United Kingdom, Germany, France, Finland, Sweden, Poland, Hong Kong S.A.R., Denmark, and Estonia. Availability depends on local telecom regulations and the availability of phone numbers.

The cost for a SkypeIn phone number at the time of this writing is 30 euros for 12 months (about a dollar a week depending on the exchange rate at the time of purchase).

One big difference with this feature is that those who are trying to reach you through this phone number do not know whether you are on line. (Remember that others using Skype who you share contact status with you know when you are online, similar to IM.) To deal with this limitation, Skype offers free voice mail with the SkypeIn service. To record your outgoing voice-mail announcement, choose **Tools > Options** on the Skype client and click the **Call Forwarding & Voicemail** icon, as shown in Figure 16-4.

Figure 16-4   Setting Up Voice Mail and Call Forwarding with Skype

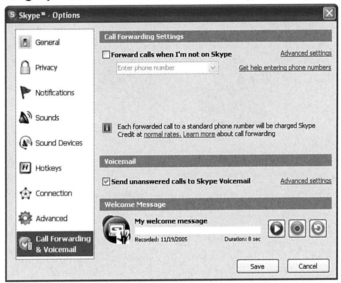

When you have a voice mail, you receive an alert (which can be an audio or visual alert, or both).

Skype is a great tool, and if you have teenagers, they are probably already using it. In fact, this should be your first troubleshooting step if you ever have trouble with Skype: Find a teenager and ask him for help.

Some businesses are considering using Skype, and while it might be good for collaboration, we would not recommend it for customer calls due to its intermittent quality (much more so than standard VoIP). Try it and you'll like it. If you have loved ones overseas or just far away, it can be a life-saver (and dollar saver).

Installing and Using Google Talk

Just as with Skype, installing Google Talk is easy. Here we review some of the differences in installation and usage. At the time of this writing, Google Talk was a limited-release beta, so some of the features might have changed by the time you read this book. We are including a discussion here because Google has been aggressive in expanding services and functionality, so it's a good bet that Google will be one of the major players in this space.

To install the program, go the Google Talk page (http://www.google.com/talk). At the time of publication, Gmail and Google Talk only work on the Windows operating system. Accessing Google Talk is shown in Figure 16-5. Go to Google, click **More**, and then click **Talk**.

Figure 16-5   Accessing Google Talk

One of the big differences between Google Talk and the other VoIP chat clients is that to sign up for an account, you first need to get a Googlemail (Gmail) account. To get a Gmail account, you need to send a Short Message Service (SMS) (text message) to a mobile phone. You can also get an invite from an existing Gmail user if you don't have a phone.

Google states on its website that the reason for the text message is to manage the number of e-mail accounts per phone and to allow it to "provide services" (read it wants to sell you stuff through your phone). No worries though; just be sure to deselect the check box that says its OK to market to you through your phone. Type your mobile number into the box, and a numeric code is sent to you on your mobile phone using SMS.

When you receive the SMS message, you can set up a Gmail account. Although you might already have at least one (and maybe several) e-mail accounts, Gmail is worth considering, because it provides a ton of free storage (2.5 GB), offers some great search options (it is Google after all), and allows you to easily import all your contacts from most of the major e-mail programs to simplify startup.

If you already have Gmail, you can sign up for Google Talk by typing in your username and password at http://www.google.com/talk.

After you install the program, the Google Talk client appears on your desktop, as shown in Figure 16-6. At this point, it works much like your typical IM program.

Figure 16-6   Google Talk Client Interface

Adding Contacts in Google Talk

One of the more innovative components of Google Talk is the way that it allows you to add friends. When you click the **Add friend** link at the bottom of the client, a small wizard pops up. You can type in the e-mail address of a friend or choose someone from your Gmail contacts list. When you choose a contact, she is sent an invitation to Google Talk. If the contact does not currently have a Gmail account, she is invited to join both Gmail and Google Talk. Again, this program was in beta status when this book was written.

 Creating a new contact database every time you start using a new program can be a drag. We prefer programs that automatically "harvest" your contacts from your existing contact database. For example, when you install Skype, it can automatically search through your contacts database, match e-mail addresses to the Skype subscriber database, and automatically add matches to your Skype contact list.

Using Google Talk

At this point, Google Talk works just like Skype does between two users. At the time of publication, however, Google Talk did not support incoming or outgoing calls to/from the PSTN, VoIP phones, or mobile phones.

We have also noticed a bit better voice quality using Skype, probably because of its advanced codec (this is the compression that digitizes and compresses your voice for transport).

We're not saying that Google Talk won't catch up, but at this point, they are behind, particularly with regard to expanding to other voice systems.

Summary

All signs point to Skype as being one of the dominant VoIP chat programs. With the emergence of SkypeIn and SkypeOut and eBay's acquisition of Skype, if you use Skype, you will probably be in the mainstream. Other players are out there, though, and players such as Google should not be counted out. Multiservice programs (VoIP chat Trillion equivalents, for example) might also emerge, lessening the impact of choosing one flavor of VoIP chat over another (unless you pick something really obscure).

Regardless of what you choose, though, we think that VoIP chat is one of the most underrated communication advances in many years, from a convenience, cost, and usefulness standpoint.

CHAPTER 17

The Future of Telephony

We end this book with what we see as the future of telephony. This is a summary of what leading industry analysts think, with a bit of speculation from the authors just for kicks.

A Review of What We Have Now

At this point in the book, many of you have already installed a VoIP system in your home as either a complete replacement of your public switched telephone network (PSTN) phone or as a PSTN add-on for free long-distance. Many of you also have a cell/mobile phone as well as a phone or private extension at work. That's three and maybe even four different phones, on four different systems.

The good news is that despite the fact that all of these phones use different systems, all the systems can "talk" to each other. The bad news is that you have three, four, or even five different numbers, more than a handful of different handsets, and several bills.

Some additional good news is that costs continue to trend downward. Now even we know that you can't get much lower than free, but many of the systems that are not free are being forced to lower their costs or risk losing all or most of their business to the free services. While this is good for consumers, you should be aware of some issues, as described in the next section.

The Cost Battle: Consumers Versus Companies and Governments

We mentioned earlier that long-distance is free over VoIP for two reasons. One reason is that VoIP calls primarily use the Internet for transport, with gateways to the PSTN when needed to complete a call to a PSTN subscriber. As a result, it is often less expensive to carry VoIP calls. It is also typically cheaper for VoIP providers to offer a lot of features, such as call waiting, caller ID, and so on, compared to upgrading a PSTN central office switch with the same features.

Another reason that VoIP is so cheap is because VoIP, which is a service on a data network, is not regulated (yet) as a voice communication and is therefore not subject to state, local, township, hamlet, regional, provincial, national, hemispherical, or galactic taxes, which tend to add up quickly.

Of these two reasons, the lack of taxable revenues is the one thing you should worry about if you have become accustomed to very low phones bills. New business models have a habit of wiping out existing companies that cannot keep up with faster, leaner startups that undercut the more expensive old guard. This is Business 101, and it's a darn good model. Governments, on the other hand, are going to get their money. You can bank on it. At the time of publication, several pieces of legislation were being introduced at several levels of government (in multiple countries), taking a serious look at whether VoIP should be regulated as a phone service, and more importantly, how to stem the tide of decreasing tax revenues.

It is a good bet, therefore, to expect that sooner or later the rates will probably go up on VoIP services (because of telecom taxes), or at least the VoIP services will maintain their current level as the providers drop their prices as the taxes are levied.

So while the cat is out of the bag on free or nearly free transport of VoIP packets, rest assured that governments will find a way to collect cash from it. It's why most governments exist in the first place.

In summary, VoIP prices might move up a bit, and other systems (such as cellular) could come down in price. The two might never "meet in the middle" but they will get close. The difference in the end might be about cost, services, and reach.

System Convergence

In addition to the costs leveling off because of taxes, most experts agree that a combining of systems will occur through mergers and the acquisitions of companies, the development of devices that work on multiple systems, or most likely, a combination of both.

The system convergence piece is easy to see. A general consolidation of media and communication companies is occurring, and soon, fewer telecom companies will exist. Each company will offer more bundled services, such as the packages that Time Warner Media offers in the United States, with broadband Internet access, VoIP, and digital cable combined for single monthly rate. Verizon is another company that started from a different space (as a PSTN provider) but is making moves toward becoming a media giant.

Still another view is from the VoIP equipment and infrastructure providers. To give you an idea of the landscape change here, in 2005, Cisco Systems became the world's number one phone system equipment provider (not just VoIP, but all telephony) after less than five years in this space and with no attempts to sell the old type of systems.

Similar to the VoIP services, the devices are also undergoing a convergence trend, whereby a single device will be the phone that you use for most communications. We look at a possible scenario in the next section.

Future Use Scenario

Imagine that you are working as a marketing manager for a high-tech company. Your job requires you to travel often, but you can work at home from time to time when not traveling. So you split your nontravel time between the corporate office and your home office. You also like to occasionally work from the local coffee shop, which has free WiFi (wireless LAN) service but lousy cell-phone coverage.

Perhaps you start the day in the home office, checking voice mail from the speakerphone on your desk, which is connected to a VoIP service from your Internet provider. You have more messages than you anticipated, so you pick up the small portable phone from the base just as you would with a cordless phone. This phone, however, connects over your wireless router rather than the cordless base. At this point, you are still routing the call through your VoIP provider.

You grab a cup of coffee and jump in the car, setting your phone in the hands-free cradle. As you pull out of your garage, the phone senses that you are leaving the usable range of your home wireless system, so it scans for a known network and finds a strong signal from your cellular provider's network. The phone immediately switches to the cellular system, seamlessly handing the call over from your VoIP network to the cellular network without so much as a blip.

After you finish with your voice mail, you receive a call from your spouse (who dialed your cell-phone number). Your phone rings and you answer it as you pull into the parking lot of your office. You pick up the phone and walk into the office. As you walk down the hall to your office, the call connects to the corporate wireless LAN system in the office, and the call is transferred to the phone system in the office. This is all transparent to both parties on the call.

After an hour or two at the office, you head to the airport. You will be gone for several days, so you open your communication manager software and set up your "follow me" mode, which routes all incoming calls to the first available of the following numbers:

1. Office number (for when you are in the office)

2. Home number (in case you are working from home)

3. Cell-phone number (while in the car)

4. Skype number (in case you are working from the coffee shop)

Any call coming in to any of those numbers will always be routed in that order.

If you are not available at any of those numbers, the caller will be prompted to leave you a voice mail. If the voice mail is marked as urgent, you will be prompted with an urgent alert as soon as you activate your phone on any of the systems (work, WLAN, home VoIP, cellular, or Skype). The voice mail will also be sent to you as an e-mail attachment.

You would also have the option of listing yourself as "busy," which would automatically route all your calls directly to voice mail, unless the call was from certain (previously identified) numbers, such as your spouse, boss, or bookie. A call from these numbers would always get through to you as long as you are on an available system.

After you are on your flight, the crew informs you that it is now safe to use approved electronics. You cannot use your cellular phone on the plane (not yet anyway, although there are proposals to allow this), but you are in business class, which has Internet access (Lufthansa currently offers this, and many other airlines are in the process of incorporating it into their planes), so you open your laptop and turn on your Skype client. You are now open for business at 35,000 feet. While checking e-mail, your Skype client rings: It's your five-year-old calling to tell you she lost her first tooth. The video client pops ups and you can see a choppy, yet viewable, live video of your suddenly much cuter kid with a missing front tooth.

Day in the Life: The Not-So-Distant Future for VoIP Services

The voice quality of Skype (on the plane) is pretty lousy (after all, you are on a shared satellite connection while flying at 400 mph above the ocean), so instead of listening to your voice mail in this mode, you download your e-mail during the in-flight movie and listen to the audio voice mail files before landing in Frankfurt.

We could go on, but you get the point. Now this might seem pretty far-fetched to some, but the reality is that we are not that far away from this scenario today. In fact, the technology is essentially available, so it is all possible. Some issues, however, need to be overcome to make it practical. The previous figure provides a diagram of the day in the life of a phone user in a similar scenario.

In summary, here are the features of this future system:

- **Presence**—The system (with your permission) will know how and where to find you, routing voice communication to the "highest level" available to you.

- **Convergence**—Lots of systems, fewer devices. Perhaps you will use a single device that works on all systems.

- **Preferred formats**—Voice or video, realtime or delayed. On this system, you will be able to read your voice mails and hear your e-mails. You will be able to see and be seen as well as hear and be heard. Commercial tag lines might switch to "Can you see me now?"

Mitigating Factor No. 1: Intrasystem Cooperation

For the scenario described in the preceding paragraphs to work, a call must be seamlessly handed off between systems; this is pretty tricky. Dual-mode phones can work across multiple systems (such as cellular, and cordless PTSN), but as of today, you cannot maintain a session (that is, stay on a call) as you switch from one system to another. To overcome this problem, different companies will need to work together to develop the tools, procedures, and legal agreements to make this all seamless.

Another issue is billing. Telecommunication companies are businesses, and they need to collect revenues to stay in business. If a device can seamlessly switch between systems, each voice provider that you use will want you to stay on its system so that it can collect revenues (even if the performance would be better on another system). Without some good rules regarding how and when calls are handed off from one system to another, you could end up "ping-ponging" among systems. This could impact your call quality, battery life, and more importantly, your phone bill (in a bad way).

One of the likely solutions to these issues is the convergence trend we mentioned earlier. If you subscribe to a service from a company that offers VoIP, cellular, and long-distance transport (such as Verizon), no conflicts of interest exist among the different access modes. It is advantageous for such companies to switch your call off of a more expensive PSTN or cellular connection, which consumes valuable telecom resources, to a cheaper Internet-based connection, which is far less expensive to operate. The advantage that these companies have will drive other companies to merge or cooperate, ultimately driving standards that gain wide adoption. We expect this all to happen over a three- to seven-year period.

Mitigating Factor No. 2: Battery Life and Size

Another factor in making this all practical is the size of the phone and the battery life. Not many people will want one of these multimode phones if it's the size of a 1980s-era cell phone (remember those giant "bag phones"?).

The issue here is that the more systems your phone works with, the more electronics you need to stuff inside the thing. You will also need to have good battery life if you are going to carry this phone around with you as you are globetrotting and trendsetting.

The good news here, of course, is that technology tends to get small and then get cheap (and by cheap, we mean a decrease in price, not necessarily quality). Figure 17-1 shows the ever-shrinking size of cell phones and the ever-growing list of capabilities and battery life.

Figure 17-1 Shrinking Cell Phone Sizes over the Years

Some good news on this front is that the telecom carriers tend to subsidize the price of the phone in exchange for you signing a long-term contract with them. It's worth it for them to lock you in, but because it's easy now to keep your old phone number even when you change carriers, the carriers try their best to keep you as a customer through good, feature-rich, and inexpensive service plans.

Conclusion

We hope this summary gives you a good idea of where telephony is going over the next few years. The short version here is that smaller phones will work in more places for less money.

As far as using VoIP in your home, we hope that this book has not only helped you set up your system but also taught you a thing or two about the new system, the old system, and how they all work together. If you got a laugh or two along the way, or were even mildly entertained, so much the better.

CHAPTER 18

From the Geek Squad Files

VoIP chat rocks! There is no other way to say it. If you like instant messaging (IM), you will love VoIP chat. The big thing here is that you need to get everyone you chat with on the same service because VoIP programs are not cross-compatible. Skype users can only talk with other Skype users, and Google Talk users can only talk with Google Talk users.

Consider the following feature ratings for VoIP chat systems:

- **Quality**—The sound quality on these systems varies considerably. Who cares though? It's free and it works, so when you have understanding folks on each end of the call, you can talk away.

- **Cost**—It's free regardless of whether you are talking to someone in the same building or across the world (on the same service, that is). That price is tough is to beat. The equipment can also be free, but you should probably use an earbud so that those around you don't hear both sides of the conversation. You can spend some money on equipment if you're so inclined, but that's an option, not a requirement.

- **Fun**—It's a blast! First of all, the implications for online gaming are staggering. You can focus on killing Klingons, Goblins, or any being that must be eliminated instead of typing messages into the game's chat window. With some of these systems, you can make the equivalent of a conference call, so you can get the entire team on the same bridge and really stomp your opponents. For you more-social types, you can send talk requests to people all over the world. (You should monitor your kids to make sure that strange adults are not trying to strike up chats with them, though.)

- **Portability**—Unlike VoIP services like cable VoIP and broadband phone services, VoIP chat services are portable. Anywhere you can take your laptop and get an Internet connection, you can make a phone call. It's very cool, but keep in mind that a cell phone is smaller and might be less expensive than paying wireless LAN hotspot usage fees.

- **Potential trouble**—The potential for getting into trouble at work can be fairly high, depending on who your buddies are. If you have friends who like to start IM or voice chat conversations with some amount of vulgarity, you should disable your chat client while giving presentations to executives, customers, or other groups at work. Not everyone shares the same sense of humor.

Numerics

911   Emergency number in the United States.

2.4 GHz   Operating frequency shared by cordless telephones, wireless home networks (802.11b/g WiFi), and unfortunately, microwave ovens and other devices that can cause interference.

5.8 GHz   Operating frequency for newer cordless telephones and wireless home networks (802.11a WiFi), with less interference (so far) from other devices.

A-B

bandwidth   The speed or capacity of data transfers across a network or a portion of a network.

binary   A numbering system based on 1s and 0s. This is the basis for all computer languages.

bit   Short for *binary digit;* this is a single digit of information, which is a 1 or 0.

broadband   A term used to describe high-speed Internet service. The term comes from the fact that a broad range of frequencies are used to attain high information exchange rates.

browser   A program used to access content on the Internet.

byte   A standard-size "chunk" of computer language or network information. A byte is comprised of 8 bits.

C

cable   Can refer to a wire with connectors to connect two devices, or can refer to the type of broadband service you get from your cable TV provider.

CALEA (Communications Assistance for Law Enforcement Agencies)   All U.S. telecommunications services must have provisions for law enforcement agencies such as the police and FBI to be able to install "wiretaps" to monitor conversations.

Cat 5 (Category 5)   The standard format for Ethernet (computer network) cabling.

chat   An instant messaging session in which three or more people are often involved.

CO (central office)   The telephone switch that connects many residential and business phone lines to the public switched telephony network (PSTN), interpreting digits dialed to route calls.

codec   A device (the name is short for *coder-decoder*) that converts digital signals to analog and vice versa. Codecs come in varying qualities. A poor-quality codec results in poor sound quality on a digital phone.

D

delay   The length of time between when speech is spoken into a handset and when it is received and played out the speaker of the handset of the called person. For VoIP, the delay includes the time involved to transport the speech-carrying VoIP packets across the Internet.

demarc (demarcation line)   The imaginary dividing line between your home phone wiring (the part that you own) and the service provider's wiring (the part that it owns).

DHCP (Dynamic Host Configuration Protocol)   A protocol used by service providers and network equipment to automatically assign IP addresses from a pool rather than assigning permanent IP addresses to users.

downlink   The connection and information flow from the service provider to your computer.

DSL (digital subscriber line)   A high-speed Internet connection that uses unused frequencies on phone lines to deliver very high data rates with the use of a specialized modem.

DTMF (dual tone multifrequency)   The tones generated by a phone handset connected to the PSTN, also known as tone dialing.

dynamic IP address   Having an IP address assigned by a device in the Internet service provider's network or home network that can change each time an address is requested.

E

E911 (Enhanced 911)   Emergency service in the United States enhanced with automatic delivery of information about the caller to the agency handling the emergency call, such as name and address.

e-mail   An application used to exchange notes and files between two or more people. An e-mail is identified by the username and the service provider, such as bob@network.com.

Ethernet   A protocol that defines the rules for computer communication over certain types of networks. It is the dominant protocol in use for both home and businesses.

exchange   Another term for a central office switch in the PSTN.

F

firewall   A physical device or software program that prevents unwanted access into a private network from an outside location, or restricts access to outside locations based on user-defined rules.

FTP (File Transfer Protocol)   One of several protocols used to copy files between computers over the Internet.

G

gateway   A device that provides a link between two different types of networks. This can be a large device, such as the ones that are present in local phone offices connecting the Internet to the PSTN, or a small device, such as the ones in your home that link an analog phone to your local network.

Gb (gigabit)   1 billion bits.

GHz (gigahertz)   A radio frequency of 1 billion cycles per second.

Google   A website used to search for topics or other sites. Its popularity has made it a verb meaning "to search," such as "I googled Geek Squad."

H

hotspot   A wireless network available for use in a public place such as a coffee shop or airport.

HTTP (Hypertext Transfer Protocol)   The computer language used to retrieve information from web pages written in certain "markup" languages.

I

IM (instant messaging)   Quickly becoming one of the most popular forms of communication over the Internet and cell-phone networks.

Internet   The worldwide system of computer networks. Although many private networks connect to it, the Internet is public, cooperative, and self-sustaining.

Internet phone adapter   A device that allows you to plug in a typical home phone and converts it to use the Internet instead of the PSTN.

IP (Internet Protocol)   Defines the communication rules for devices on the Internet. Communication within this protocol is based on the assignment of IP addresses.

IP address   A numerical address by which computers, web servers, and devices are known on the Internet. IP addresses have little bearing on geographic location.

IP telephony   Telephone service provided over a data network.

ISP (Internet service provider)   A company that provides access to the Internet for residential or business use.

J–K

jitter   The result of VoIP packets arriving with significant differences in the time required to transport them end to end. Jitter can cause voice quality issues.

Kb (kilobit)   1000 bits. This is a standard transmission rate for dialup modems when referred to over a portion of time such as Kbps, or kilobits per second.

L

LAN (local-area network)   A small network within a house, department, or business.

latency   The delay in sending packets from one part of a network to another. Latency almost always refers to the delay of packets containing "voice" signals.

LED (light emitting diode)   The green, red, and amber (or other color) status indicator lights on computers and networking gear.

LNP (Local Number Portability)   Allows telephone subscribers to keep their existing telephone number when switching to a different service provider.

loss   Occurs when some percentage of VoIP packets carrying speech are sent but not received at the destination.

M-N

MAC (Media Access Control) address   The unique physical serial number given by the manufacturer to every networking device used for network communication.

Mb (megabit)   1 million bits. When measured over time, this is the standard transmission rate unit for high-speed modems.

modem (modulator-demodulator)   A device that translates computer language for transmission over a network media and back again.

MSC (mobile switching center)   Equivalent to a central office, but in the mobile telephone network.

NPAC (Number Portability Administration Center)   Keeps a large database that matches subscriber telephone numbers with the subscribers' current phone line location, making Local Number Portability possible.

P

PDA (personal digital assistant)   A small, hand-held computer such as a Palm Pilot.

peer-to-peer   Communications that occur when two computers establish a connection directly to each other without an intermediary server, gateway, or device.

ping   A utility program on most PCs that can be used to test a network connection.

POP (point of presence)   The location of Internet access, typically with reference to a service provider.

PSAP (Public Safety Answering Point)   The agency responsible for receiving emergency calls from subscribers and dispatching appropriate emergency response services, such as police, fire, and rescue. In the United States, dialing 9-1-1 on any telephone creates a call to the nearest PSAP.

PSTN (public switched telephony network)   The standard phone network we all know and love.

R

RBOC (regional Bell operating company)   One of the original Bell companies that resulted from the divestiture of the United States telephone system monopoly in the mid-1980s.

REN (Ringer Equivalence Number)   A number assigned to each phone handset to calculate the total allowable loading on a phone line interface. For example, if a phone circuit has a maximum REN value of 5 and each handset has a REN value of 1, a maximum of 5 handsets can be connected to the line.

RJ11   A telephone cable that connects a phone handset to the phone jack in your house.

RJ45   An Ethernet cable, which has a wider jack than an RJ11 cable.

router   A networking device that makes "intelligent" decisions regarding how traffic is moved across or through a network.

S

sampling   The process of taking many portions of speech waveforms each second to represent the speech in binary 1s and 0s.

signaling   The communication between phones or local phone offices during the setting up and tearing down of phone calls.

SIP (Session Initiation Protocol)   A high-level signaling protocol used to initiate interactive user sessions involving multimedia elements, including voice, video, and IM.

Skype   A popular free Internet-based voice chat service.

slamming   When a long-distance provider (or telecom provider) switches you to its service through questionable means with or sometimes without your permission. Slamming is illegal and should be reported to the FCC.

softphone   A software program running on a PC or laptop that emulates all the features of a phone. Used primarily for PC-to-PC calling, although calls can also be made to regular PSTN phones or cell phones, usually for a small fee.

softswitch   A telephone switch that processes many VoIP calls but does not physically connect to handsets like a central office switch would in the PSTN.

SSID (service set identifier)   A term used for the name of a WLAN.

static IP address   Having an IP address assigned by the Internet service provider, which does not change. Static IP addresses can be assigned to any computer on a private network.

switch   A large computerized telephone device that processes many calls simultaneously. This term is also used in networking to define a device that forwards and segments traffic though a network.

T

TA (terminal adapter)   Allows a regular telephone handset from the PSTN to be used with a VoIP service.

TCP (Transmission Control Protocol)   A network protocol and set of rules used with the Internet Protocol (IP) set of rules to send data in the form of message units between computers over the Internet. These are often just referred to as TCP/IP.

TiVo   A service that allows digital recording of live TV, also known as a DVR (digital video recorder). Warning: The authors have found TiVo to be highly addictive.

U

uplink   The data flow from a computer to a service provider (and then to the Internet).

UPS (uninterruptible power supply)   Provides backup power from a battery source during a power outage to keep computer equipment operating.

USB (Universal Serial Bus)   An interface that allows other devices to be connected and disconnected without resetting the system. Also a serial communication standard that allows high-speed data communication to many devices.

V-W-X-Y-Z

VoIP (Voice over IP)   A protocol for transporting voice conversations across a data network. Also known as IP telephony.

VoIP chat   Using the Internet for voice conversations and phone calls. You typically have no number to call, but you reach others through their "handle," much like instant messaging. Online gaming systems, such as Xbox Live, often provide a voice chat feature for players to communicate during games.

WAN (wide-area network)   A network that covers a large geographic area. When used as a proper noun, it usually refers to the Internet.

Numerics

3-3-4 system, 5
  area code, 6
  exchange prefix, 6
  line number, 6
  unusable numbers, 6
911 services
  handling calls over VoIP systems, 40, 42
  registering, 84

A

adding
  contacts to Google Talk, 137
  Internet VoIP service as a second line, 95-96
  people to Skype contact list, 131
affordability of broadband phone services, reasons for
  infrastructure costs, 25
  public telephone service taxes and fees, 26-27
  regulatory compliance, 26
  transport costs, 26
aggregation, 34
analog waveforms, converting to digital signals, 20
area code, 6
audio diagnostic messages on terminal adapters, playing, 109
audio quality, improving, 131
availability of virtual phone numbers, 31

B

backup generators, 56
bandwidth, effect on voice quality, 35
Bell System breakup, 9
  effect on phone system architecture, 11
broadband phone services, 13–14
  cable VoIP phone services, 50–51
  connection speed, effect on voice quality, 110–112
  electric powering, 22-23
  network quality, effect on voice quality, 112–114

C

cable modems, terminal adapters, 67
cable VoIP phone services, 50
  connecting, 77-78
  installing with existing house wiring, 93

  providers, 51
  selecting, 67
  test calls, performing, 83-84
call forwarding, 32
call logs, 32
carrier signal, 20
chat services, 52
  feature ratings, 145
  Google Talk
    contacts, adding, 137
    installing, 135-136
  IM, 121-122
    limitations of, 126
    translator programs, 125
  Linksys CIT200 Cordless Internet Telephony kit, 53
  providers, 53
  real-time, 121
  Skype
    available accessories, 132-133
    installing, 129-130
    placing calls, 133-134
    receiving calls, 134-135
choppy voice quality, factors affecting
  broadband network quality, 112-114
  broadband speed, 111-112
circuit switching, 15-17
click to dial, 32
client-server systems, 122
CO (central office), 6
  softswitches, 19
combining multiple VoIP services, 98-100
comfort noise, 37
comparing service plans, 62, 65
connecting
  cable VoIP service, 77-79
  cordless phones to VoIP service, 87
  Internet VoIP service, 79
connectivity issues, troubleshooting, 107-109
contacts, adding to Google Talk, 137
convergence
  impact on VoIP's future, 140-143
  intrasystem cooperation, 143
converting analog waveforms to digital signals, 20
cordless phones
  adding to VoIP services, 87
  interference with wireless network, troubleshooting, 115-117
  two-line, 88-90

cost of VoIP phone services
  as service selection criteria, 57-60
  effect of regulations on, 139-140

D

delay, effect on voice quality, 37
demarc, 91
dial tones, DTMF, 8
dialing issues, troubleshooting, 115
digital switches, 6
DSL (Digital Subscriber Line), 13
DTMF (dual-tone multifrequency), 8
dual-mode phones, 132
  intrasystem cooperation, 143

E

E911 services, 39
  calls, handling over VoIP systems, 40-42
  registering, 84
earbud-and-mic setup, 132
electric powering of broadband phone services, 22-23
electrical outages
  backup generators, 56
  UPSs, 56
emergency number services, 37
  911 calls, handling over VoIP systems, 40-42
  establishing, 84
exchange prefix, 6
extending VoIP service to multiple rooms, 106
  with wireless bridges, 103-104
  with wireless phone jacks, 104-105

F

fax machines, 101
FCC fact sheet website, 62
features of services as selection criteria, 61
five nines, 33
flat-rate service, 9
flexibility. *See* LNP, 27
Friis, Janus, 126
future of telephony, 139
  government regulations, 139-140
  system convergence, 140-143
  VoIP
    intrasystem cooperation, 143
    shrinking battery life and size, 144

G

gaming online using VoIP service, 56
Google Talk
  contacts, adding, 137
  installing, 135-136

H

handling 911 calls over VoIP systems, 40-42
headsets, 132
hierarchical telephone network design, 9
  regional centers, 9
  toll centers, 9
home alarm systems, compability with Internet telephony, 117
Home Networking Simplified, 104
home security/alarm systems, 101
home telephone wiring, 90
  grounding, 91
  junction boxes, 91

I

IM (instant messaging), 121-122
  service limitations, 126
  translator programs, 125
improving audio quality, 131
indicator lights on terminal adapters, 107-108
installing
  cable VoIP with existing house wiring, 93-95
  Google Talk, 135-136
  integrated router/terminal adapters, 81-83
  Internet VoIP service as a second line, 95-96
  Skype, 129-130
  stand-alone terminal adapters, 80-81
  two-line external splitters, 92-93
integrated router/terminal adapter, 70
  installing, 81-83
interference from cordless devices, avoiding, 117
intermittent broadband problems, troubleshooting, 114
Internet VoIP service
  adding as a second line, 95-96
  connecting, 79
  optimizing, 117
  selecting, 73
  terminal adapter, selecting, 68-72
  test calls, performing, 83-84
  two-line, 99-100
intrasystem cooperation, 143

J–K

jitter, 113
junction boxes, 91
Kazaa, 126

L

last mile, 34
latency, 113
limitations
  of broadband phone services
    cost, 45
    emergency number services, 37-39, 45
    portability issues, 39
    reliability issues, 33-34, 45
    voice quality, 35-37, 45
  of virtual phone numbers, 31
line numbers, 6
Linksys CIT200 cordless phones, 133
Linksys PAP2 terminal adapter LEDs, 107
LNP (Local Number Portability), 6, 27-29
local phone services, mobile telephone systems, 11
long-distance telephone companies, slamming, 10
maintaining
  minimal PSTN line, 57
  multiple VoIP services, 99-100
  separate PSTN and VoIP lines, 88
manual terminal adapter configuration, 85-86
measuring packet loss, 113
mobile phone system, 11
  SSPs, 12
modems (cable), terminal adapters, 67
MSCs (mobile switching centers), 12
multiple handsets on VoIP systems
  effect on audio quality, 97
  Ringer Equivalence Number, troubleshooting, 96-97

N

network quality, effect on voice quality, 112-114
number portability and emergency services, 39-40

O

offline forwarding, 32
online call management
  call forwarding, 32
  call logs, 32
  click to dial, 32
  voice mail, 31

online games, utilizing VoIP service, 56
operator-based telephone system, 3-5
optimizing Internet telephone service, 117
out-of-service forwarding, 32
overloaded REN limits, troubleshooting, 96-97

P

packet loss
  effect on voice quality, 37
  measuring, 113
packet switching, 15-17
PC-to-PC calling, 52
  Linksys CIT200 Cordless Internet Telephony kit, 53
  providers, 53
  VoIP chat system feature ratings, 145
peer-to-peer systems, 122
phone number, selecting, 80
placing calls with Skype, 133-134
Plantronics headsets, 132
power outages, UPSs, 56
public telephone system, 3
  3-3-4 system, 5-6
  Bell System breakup, 9
    effect on phone system architecture, 11
  digital switches, 6
  DTMF, 8
  hierarchical network design, 9
  home telephone wiring, 90-91
  Internet access, 13
  local phone services, mobile phone systems, 11
  long distance companies, slamming, 10
  operator-based, 3-5
  reliability of, 14, 35
  SSPs, 12
  wireless services, 11

R

RBOCs (regional Bell operating centers), 9
"real-time", 121
receiving calls with Skype, 134-135
regional centers, 9
registering
  for 911/E911 services, 84
  phone services, 78
  terminal adapters, 80
  with "do not call" list, 78
regulations, effect on VoIP phone service costs, 139-140

reliability
> as service selection criteria, 61
> five nines, 33
> of public telephone system, 14

resetting broadband connection, 109

Ringer Equivalence Number, troubleshooting overloads, 96-97

S

sampling, 20-22

satellite receiver dishes, 101

SCPs (Service Control Points), 12

selecting
> headsets, 132
> VoIP service, 80
>> *cable, 67*
>> *cost, 57-60*
>> *features, 61*
>> *Internet, 68-73*
>> *reliability, 61*
>> *specialized device support, 61-62*
>> *typical phone service applications, international calling, 55*
> phone number, 80

service connection problems, troubleshooting, 107-109

service plans
> comparing, 62, 65
> selecting, 80

signaling, 17-19
> converting analog waveforms to digital signals, 20
> sampling, 22

single-line cordless phone systems, 88

Skype, 126, 132
> available accessories, 132-133
> calls
>> *placing, 133-134*
>> *receiving, 134-135*
> installing, 129-130

SkypeIn phone numbers, 134

slamming, 10

softswitches, 19, 50

specialized phone devices
> fax machines, 101
> home security/alarm systems, 101
> satellite receiver dishes, 101
> support of as service selection criteria, 61-62
> TiVo, 101

speed of broadband connection
> effect on voice quality, 110-112
> testing, 111

splitters, effect on broadband connection, 114

SS7 (Signaling System 7), 12

SSPs (service switching points), 12

stand-alone terminal adapters, 69
> installing, 80-81

static IP addresses, manual terminal adapter configuration, 85-86

system convergence
> impact on future of VoIP, 140-143
> intrasystem cooperation, 143

T

technical support websites, 115

telecom industry consolidation, 13

Telecommunications Act of 1996, 13

telemarketing, registering with "do not call" list, 78

telephone numbers, 3-3-4 system, 5-6

"ten-minute miracle", 110

terminal adapters, 67
> audio diagnostic messages, playing, 109
> for Internet VoIP service, selecting, 68-72
> indicator lights, 107-108
> integrated router/terminal adapters, installing, 81-83
> manual configuration, 85-86
> registering, 80
> stand-alone, installing, 80-81

test calls, performing, 83-84

testing broadband connection speed, 111

TiVo, 101

toll centers, 9

toll switches, 9

Trillian, 125

troubleshooting
> audio quality, multiple handsets, 97
> dialing-related issues, 115
> multiple handsets, Ringer Equivalence Number, 96-97
> service connection problems, 107-109
> voice quality issues, 110-114
>> *cordless phone interference, 115*

true peer-to-peer networks, 122

trunks, 9

two-line cordless phone systems, 88-90

two-line external splitters, installing, 92-93

two-line Internet VoIP services, 99-100

U

unusable 3-3-4 numbers, 6

uplink speed, testing, 111

UPSs (uninterruptible power supplies), 56

V

virtual phone numbers, 29

voice mail, 31

voice quality issues, troubleshooting, 110-114

VoIP phone services, 2. *See also* **VoIP chat services**
adding cordless phones, 87
combining, 98-100
electric powering of broadband phone services, 22-23
extending to multiple rooms
with wireless bridges, 103-104
with wireless phone jacks, 104-105
multiple handsets, effect on audio quality, 97
signaling, 17-19
converting analog waveforms to digital signals, 20
sampling, 22

VoIP chat services, 52
feature ratings, 145
Google Talk
contacts, adding, 137
installing, 135-136
IM, 121-122
limitations of, 126
translator programs, 125
Linksys CIT200 Cordless Internet Telephony kit, 53
providers, 53
real-time, 121
Skype, 129-130
available accessories, 132-133
calls, placing, 133-134
calls, receiving, 134-135

VoIPReview website, 64

W-X-Y-Z

websites for technical support, 115

wireless devices, extending VoIP service to multiple rooms
bridges, 103-104
handsets, Linksys CIT200 Cordless Internet Telephony kit, 53
phone jacks, 104-105

wireless networks, troubleshooting cordless phone interference, 115

wireless services, 11–12

Zennström, Niklas, 126

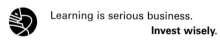